Creativity and Innovation
– the Structural Engineer's
Contribution to Design

Bill Addis

Architectural Press

Oxford • Auckland • Boston • Johannesburg • Melbourne • New Delhi

Architectural Press
An imprint of Butterworth-Heinemann
Linacre House, Jordan Hill, Oxford OX2 8DP
225 Wildwood Avenue, Woburn, MA 01801-2041
A division of Reed Educational and Professional Publishing Ltd

A member of the Reed Elsevier plc group

First published 2001

British Library Cataloguing in Publication Data
A catalogue record for this book is available from the British Library

Library of Congress Cataloguing in Publication Data
A catalogue record for this book is available from the Library of Congress

ISBN 0 7506 4210 6

www.bh.com/architecturalpress

Printed and bound in Great Britain

PLANT A TREE
British Trust for Conservation Volunteers
FOR EVERY TITLE THAT WE PUBLISH, BUTTERWORTH-HEINEMANN
WILL PAY FOR BTCV TO PLANT AND CARE FOR A TREE.

Contents

Preface

Few building clients or architects are fully aware of what structural engineers can contribute to their buildings. This book is intended for all those who would know more about what structural engineers do and how they can enhance the value of buildings for their owners, architects and users. It illustrates how much more creative engineers can contribute to architecture than implied by the stereotypical image of the engineer as calculator or provider of connection details. The book is also intended for young engineers who, fresh from their mathematical and scientific university courses, are just beginning to put this knowledge to good use. It aims to demonstrate the links between the engineer's understanding of structural materials, form and behaviour, and the products, the performance and the quality that his or her clients require. The book is also intended to help young architects better understand how good engineers can help them realise their projects, especially when involved from the very beginning. Getting the best input from engineers is often a matter of knowing what sort of input to ask for.

The book has many origins.

Since I was a student I have been saddened that students of civil and structural engineering were not encouraged to take an active interest in design, despite the fact that this is the principal engineering activity that they undertake after graduation. This is in stark contrast with students of architecture. Many of those who become engineers have done so mainly because of a talent for maths and physics at school, not as the result of an enthusiasm for designing, innovating and making things.

This book aims to convey the innovation and creative thinking that is truly the basis of every aspect and every stage of the engineer-

Art is solving problems which cannot be formulated before they have been solved. The search goes on, until a solution is found, which is deemed to be satisfactory. There are always many possible solutions, the search is for the best – but there is no best – just more or less good.

Ove Arup

ing design of buildings. The engineer's creativity and ability to innovate is poorly understood. I hope to convey something of the value that can be generated for clients and architects from innovation in engineering. Indeed, in the construction industry, alone amongst manufacturing industries, innovation is seen as something to be avoided. It is seen only as increasing risk to the client. In fact the opposite is more often true in the hands of good engineers who, time and again, innovate in order to reduce risk. Engineering innovation is also perceived as adding costs to a project. In fact devising new ways of building is often the principal way that construction costs can be reduced. Furthermore, focusing only on costs also ignores the value that innovation can bring for the client.

The quantity surveyor's common practice of relying on historic costing can also make it very difficult to communicate the benefits of innovative engineering – if something is new there can be no historic cost data. Similarly the tendering process often discriminates against innovative engineering design. When faced with a non-standard

design, most contractors increase their prices. It requires dogged determination on the part of a design engineer to persuade a contractor to collaborate in demonstrating that a non-standard design and construction method can be less costly or quicker or more likely to finish on time. There is a very broad spectrum to 'innovation' in structural engineering – from devising a connection that uses one bolt fewer than usual to spanning an unprecedented area of floor space or devising an entirely new way of making buildings earthquake resistant. Firms that are set up to be able to challenge orthodoxy can assess when a standard solution is most appropriate and when there are benefits to be gained from innovation. Clients, architects, quantity surveyors or project managers are entirely unable to make reliable judgements about these matters without leadership from engineers.

All this illustrates the many ways in which the activity of engineering design can often be rendered invisible, and it can be difficult for outsiders to understand just what design engineers do. In a world now dominated by marketing and creating an image, it is vital that engineers devote more of their energies to publicising the nature of their skills in order to sell their services. Unfortunately, most design engineers seem to be too busy designing, too modest to undertake self-publicity or lacking in communication skills, or all three.

Engineers are in a vicious circle. They are often allocated insufficient time to do really good engineering design, and so the buildings that get built do not provide the client with as much added value as they might have got, had the engineers had more time to design a better building. It is thus often assumed that engineers contribute little value to buildings. While better buildings can be delivered to clients by applying all manner of management techniques to the design and the construction processes, it is important to remember that the best way to get better buildings is for clients to employ good designers and to allow them enough time to think carefully about every aspect of the design – including how the building will be built and maintained – before construction begins.

This vicious circle will only be broken by design engineers themselves: others have vested interests in perpetuating it. Engineers must ensure everybody knows what they do to make projects happen. We must ensure architects and contractors do not continue taking all the credit for buildings by getting on with the publicity themselves. And we must not only publicise the buildings but also what the engineers' contributions were, for otherwise people continue with their assumption that architects and contractors did it all!

But things are changing. Engineers and engineering are again becoming more prominent in the public eye, and not just when something goes wrong. All university engineering courses now have design projects and there are now several national awards for student engineering design projects. In schools the curriculum now contains Design and Technology from the age of 11 up to 16 and even beyond. Recently there have been many more television and radio programmes about both modern and historical engineering. In 1998 the Pompidou Centre in Paris held an exhibition on 'The Art of the Engineer'. London's Design Museum has recently put on the first major exhibition about I.K. Brunel, probably Britain's most famous engineer who devised the Saltash Bridge, the Great Western Railway, the Great Eastern ship and much more besides. And the MacRobert Award – the engineers' equivalent of the Turner Prize for sculpture, or the Booker prize for literature – has recently gained greater prominence since it was awarded to the engineers who designed the Millennium Dome in Greenwich which, amid the unfortunate publicity about its contents, is surely one of the greatest engineering achievements of the twentieth century. And at long last, the entry that the Yellow Pages in Britain used to contain – 'Boring – see Civil Engineers' – has been removed.

There has also been a growing awareness by some architects and building clients of the tangible benefits that can be attained by employing good engineers to develop imaginative solutions in the unique circumstances that surround all major, and many minor building projects. Creative design and innovation in construction is slowly coming to be regarded rather more as it is in the automotive or electronics industry – a means for achieving products which perform better, which better meet the users' needs, which incur less risk to the parties involved and which generate better value for money.

This transformation has come about partly through clients' pressure to get more for their money, and partly because many consulting engineers are becoming more adept at conveying the benefits of their input to projects, especially in their early stages. There has also been an increasing sophistication of engineering design methods and the computing tools available to engineers. It is now possible to model many more of the complexities of building engineering systems than a decade ago. This allows a much more thorough exploration of different alternatives at concept and scheme design stages, as well as greater confidence in the results of such investigations.

As the technical performance of buildings increases, so the different engineering systems must be conceived and developed with more and more interaction and integration. It is increasingly common for structural, civil and services engineers to collaborate closely at

concept design stage – an approach that has long been the norm for high-performance machines such as cars, aircraft and ships. These trends will inevitably continue and spread throughout the building construction industry. While many of the projects in this book are large and of higher prestige than the 'average' building, it is important to recognise that significant progress and innovation in engineering is often achieved on such projects because the rewards are so much greater. Once achieved, innovations can then spread quickly to other, more modest projects. This occurs most easily, of course, if the same design engineers are employed, for, despite the considerable progress in engineering science and calculation methods during the last century or so, much engineering skill and expertise resides in individuals and can be gained only by actually doing it and learning how to do it better next time.

For too long, perhaps, engineers have undervalued their ability to solve problems that no-one else can solve. They tend to take the attitude 'we'll just get on and do it', without realising that in doing so they make it look simple to non-engineers and hence appear to be of less value. Engineers should spend more time emphasising how

difficult their work is, not how easy it is. This poses a challenge for many engineers involved in building design whose education and professional training have tended to ignore the cost and value implications of their design work for the client. But the tide is turning. Those engineering design firms that are able to manage effectively the processes of research, innovation and design development, and the associated financial and risk issues, are becoming more noticeable for their commercial success. Even in the decade since I began compiling this book's antecedent *The Art of the Structural Engineer*, the nature of examples of good structural engineering design has changed. No longer is the structure often seen as a separate aspect of a building; it is part of an integrated whole which better meets the client's needs. The structure of this new book aims to reflect these developments.

Finally, this book has come about because of my own enthusiasms for structures, materials and engineering design which began when very young, designing and making machines with Meccano and buildings with Bayko. This had been inspired mainly by my father, but also publications from an age now gone – the Meccano Magazine, the cutaway how-it-works pictures in the Eagle comic and classic books from the 1930s with such marvellous titles as *Engineering Wonders of the World* and *The Wonder Book of Engineering Wonders*. Here you could see pictures of 'natives using long-stroke riveting hammers for bridge construction in India' and of 'the Bucyrus steam shovel holding thirty-four men', and read of 'the romance of the lifting magnet' and of 'the engineer as builder' who, in 1904, was able to erect 'the steel cage of the New Phelan Building, San Francisco (329 by 296 by 205 feet) … in seventy-five working days'. A crucial difference between these old books and what we find today is that the engineering artefacts were always portrayed as the products of man's efforts, skills and progress. There was no mention of the impersonal thing called 'technology' which we nowadays hear is responsible for all our aircraft, computers, cars, bridges and buildings. As engineers we must never cease reminding the public and politicians of our vital role in creating the very world we live in.

I have learnt a great deal about modern engineering and the nature of engineering design from studying engineering history and I think it is important that all engineers should have some knowledge of the great achievements in their field, not only to avoid reinventing the wheel, but also to develop a better sense of professional identity and pride. It is ironic that so many great buildings from the past survive, yet so few people know the names of the engineers involved in their creation. All structural engineers should know Wren's roof truss at the Sheldonian theatre in Oxford (1669), our cast-iron frame, high-rise factory buildings of the early 1800s, culminating in Fairbairn's Saltaire Mill (1853), our enormous wrought-iron railway stations of the 1850s and 1860s, the magnificent reinforced concrete roof over the Jahrhunderthalle at Breslau (1912), the breakthroughs in steel frame buildings in Britain made by Sven Bylander at the Ritz Hotel (1906) and by Felix Samuely at Simpsons of Piccadilly (1934), and the many remarkable structures by Luigi Nervi and Eduardo Torroja in the 1950s. Even more recent classics such as the Sydney Opera House (1960) and the Pompidou Centre in Paris (1975) might be familiar names, but few people are nowadays aware of the reasons these buildings are important milestones in the story of the ever-developing art of the structural engineer. In a sense, then, this is also a history book – some examples of recent precedent to help designers develop a wider vocabulary to augment their own structural language.

Bill Addis May 2001

Some philosophy

Creativity and Innovation – the Structural Engineer's Contribution to Design is about what structural designers do and how they do it well. One barrier to understanding any skill is that those who can do it well make it look easy. This book tries to convey what it is that engineers do which seems to be so difficult for non-engineers to appreciate.

It is many people's perception that structural engineers merely ensure that an architect's design for a building will stand up and be safe, and that this involves a process requiring a great many calculations of stresses and deflections. Engineers do indeed do this, but they do much more besides. Architect and structural engineer usually work together closely during the entire process of developing the design of a building from the early concept stage through to the level of fine detail and construction. They are equal parents to their child and, like all parents, they make different contributions.

Another misconception is that engineering design has a certain inevitability about it – if it is based on scientific laws, how can there be any room for choice and subjectivity? This notion is reinforced by all the rational explanations and calculations which engineers need to produce as justification for their various decisions. But the convergence and objectivity of these later stages only commence after the earlier, highly divergent and turbulent stage of the design process during which all members of the design team propose, compare, reject and develop alternative ideas.

The engineer creatively combines various threads of thought, some contradictory and incompatible, to arrive at a specific product.

Structure

You cannot have an engineering structure which is not made of a material, nor a material which is not in the form of a structure. It was Galileo, in 1638, who first clearly distinguished these two concepts and introduced the idea of stress in a material. He used them to argue against the view held 'by very many intelligent people' that the strength of a rope diminishes with its length. These people were, of course, correct, but not for the right reason. He exposed this fallacy by distinguishing between the weakness in a rope due to smaller area of cross-section and one due to fibres of an inferior quality: a longer rope is usually weaker than a shorter one because there is a higher probability of it containing one of these weaknesses, not simply because it is longer.

Robert Hooke followed some forty years later with his famous law and introduced the concept of the stiffness of a material, as distinct from a structure made of that material. More recently, the waters have become rather muddied again with composite materials such as fibreglass and concrete containing steel bars, and with our knowledge of molecules. At the atomic scale all materials are structures, rather like a great many balls linked by springs. At the millimetre scale a material may be considered as entirely homogenous; in turn, pieces of a material may be linked together to form a structure such as a truss or fabric. Finally, if the truss or fabric is of sufficient extent, it may be convenient to think of it once again as homogenous.

Structure is all about doing more with less – using less material to support a given load or enclose a given volume, or making a

The profession [of structural engineering] does not attract young people because it is considered to be neither high-tech nor creative – though it is, unlike any other profession, both.

Jörg Schlaich

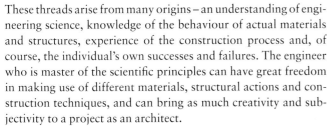

Art I assume to be any direction of the practical intellect to making things.

Alan Harris

These threads arise from many origins – an understanding of engineering science, knowledge of the behaviour of actual materials and structures, experience of the construction process and, of course, the individual's own successes and failures. The engineer who is master of the scientific principles can have great freedom in making use of different materials, structural actions and construction techniques, and can bring as much creativity and subjectivity to a project as an architect.

Later in the book we look at how structural engineers helped to create some of the buildings they have worked on. But first, let us explore the nature of our subject a little with some talk of structure, which means different things to different people; of the nature of structural design, which is different from design carried out by an architect; of the sometimes harmonious, sometimes discordant relationship between engineer and architect; and of why some structures are acclaimed as good structures, others not.

stiffer or stronger object without using more material. Many structural engineers are fascinated by the whole idea of minimum weight structures, though they are generally used only in special circumstances such as aerospace structures or long-span roofs. More often it is a matter of balancing structural performance with the cost of achieving it; many more resources are needed to design and manufacture a structure with less weight, and this follows the law of diminishing returns – saving the first 10 per cent is easier than the next.

Structure is also a matter of scale. All manner of properties change as structures get bigger (Galileo helped us understand this too) and they do not all change at the same rate. Many an architect has been disappointed to learn that the balsa-wood and card structure he has made will not work when the span becomes many tens of metres.

Finally, structure is about choosing appropriate materials which can be made into suitable pieces and joined together so that the different elements are linked to form an effective whole.

We all have a feel for structure, but we cannot experience it directly like a smell. We can feel load through our muscles, although this can be misleading since our muscles get tired whereas loads and structures do not. We can sense movement too, either visually or through our sense of touch and the kinaesthetic feelings in our limbs. It might be argued that we can sense stress in some circumstances: a force applied by a drawing pin will cause pain but by a thumb will not; yet a sharp needle can sometimes penetrate the flesh without causing pain.

Our sense of structure comes from combining primary sensations and somehow interpreting them. Thus, we can sense stiffness as a relationship between force and movement, stability as a relationship between the weight of an object and the force needed to overturn it. Similarly, we build up a picture of structural or material properties such as strength, ductility and brittleness, the instability of a strut or even the structural advantages of folding a thin sheet. We come to know such things when we are very young, playing with wooden blocks and paper aeroplanes. We need to prove nothing to ourselves – 'I know that steel is stronger than timber' – but we cannot impart this knowledge to someone else.

Although we may all have such a feel for structure, we might not be conscious of it. Some of us may have developed a better sense of structure than others, but we might find it difficult to talk about such a skill. It is interesting to note this lay feel for structures in various words for flying buttress: German – *Strebebogen* (striving

order is spatial, musical or verbal. While anyone can perceive a structure, it starts to get interesting when we look at who is perceiving it and how they think and talk about the perception, and how they remember it or store it in the form of knowledge. Perceiving a structure is an active process and utterly dependent on the eye and brain of the person involved.

Even perceiving structure as geometry can involve interpretation. Ellipses, squares, cones and pyramids have geometric properties which are not immediately apparent to the untrained eye, such as how they can be easily subdivided and how they might appear from a different viewpoint. There are also relationships within and between shapes such as symmetry, proportion, harmony, and the consequences of two shapes intersecting. Shapes have cultural significance too. Triangles and circles have long been linked with an idea of perfection, both in a religious context and elsewhere. Certain geometric proportions were seen by Greek and medieval philosophers as the key to explaining the way the world worked, much as we nowadays use physics, biology and chemistry to explain natural phenomena. Geometrical forms can remind us of other artefacts with those shapes. In a building an architect might wish to evoke something by association – a floor structure similar to the jack-arch structures ubiquitous in 19th-century warehouses and mills, or a Roman barrel vault – with no intention that it should work structurally in the original manner.

To see a structure in geometrical terms is to be able to build a mathematical model of it and be able to manipulate and test it in an abstract way. Over the last few centuries mathematicians and

The positive role for the engineers' genius and skill [is] to use their understanding of materials and structure to make real the presence of the materials in use in the building, so that people warm to them, want to touch them, feel a sense of the material itself and of the people who made and designed it. To do this we have to avoid the worst excesses of the industrial hegemony. To maintain the feeling that it was the designer, and not industry and its available options, that decided, is one essential ingredient of seeking a tactile, <u>traces de la main</u> solution.

Peter Rice

  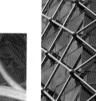  

arc); French – *arc boutant* (pushing arc); Spanish – *arbotante* (throwing arc).

We all experience structures in other ways too. We can see the materials they are made of, how strong they are and how light. We can see their form, both in man-made and naturally occurring structures such as trees, shells and flower petals. At one level we perceive these simply as geometrical shapes; at another we might imbue them with qualities of cultural, historical or psychological significance. We might also interpret them in terms of the concepts of engineering science.

Structure, then, is an abstract quality. It needs presence in the real world to be fully apprehended – what the structure is made of is important, as is where it is, what it is doing and who is apprehending it. Structure, in a general sense, is a relationship between various entities which displays a certain order and lack of randomness. To perceive order requires intelligence, whether the

scientists have invented another branch of mathematics – statics – in terms of which we can build other models of real-world objects. These models are founded, first of all, on geometry, but also contain information about loads and properties of materials so that they can simulate the response of materials to loads. This formal language of statics employs precisely defined concepts such as force, stress and stiffness, and various structural paradigms such as beams, arches and trusses. And here is where the difficulties and confusions can begin, for most of these concepts share words with our everyday language. The engineer's beam or arch is far more precisely and mathematically defined than the everyday word; conversely, what a non-engineer describes as an arch, beam or truss may, or may not, work as such in the engineer's sense of the word. Even two engineers may differ – one may describe a structure as a stiffened arch, another as a curved truss; they might even use different mathematical models to investigate its structural behaviour.

Architect and engineer will, then, interpret what they see in a structure in different ways – and these differences are not superficial. Their concept of structures is different and this affects the very thoughts and ideas they are likely to have. An architect will tend to conceive building forms either in terms of simple geometric shapes such as arcs, squares, spheres, cylinders and planes, and various man-made objects, or in terms of natural forms, which usually cannot be defined using simple geometry – bubbles, leaves, flowers, bones, ripples and so on.

Engineers, in addition, have their own set of preferred geometric forms which have their origins in the mathematical models found in structural science. An I- or an inverted T-shape are efficient cross-sections for a beam; depending on the material and how it is manufactured, efficient cross-sections for a column might be a solid circle, a tube, an H or a ✛. In order to use the minimum amount of material, beams and columns should taper as a parabola or paraboloid from their centres to the ends. Trusses need to be made up of triangles, sometimes of identical shape and size, sometimes changing. Suspension structures (and arches, inverted) feature catenaries or parabolas. Shells are usually made in the form of paraboloids, hyperboloids or hyperbolic paraboloids, but may also be elliptical, spherical, cylindrical or even have the form of a Lemniscate of Bernoulli (as in the Bank of England printing works at Debden).

A common thread among these engineers' forms is that they seldom occur naturally to architects – and even if they do, they are likely to be favoured for their geometry rather than their structural

would, for instance, be difficult to appreciate the significance of the difference between statically determinate and indeterminate (redundant) structures. This is especially true of the difference between bracing a structure by triangulation as opposed to portal or Vierendeel action, or the idea that particularly stiff parts of a structure attract load away from other less stiff load paths through a structure. It might be possible to understand the differences between linear and non-linear materials: most materials are linear while they remain elastic in compression and tension, steel becomes non-linear when it deforms in a ductile way in tension or compression. A stone wall and a cable are both non-linear in another way; the first will carry compression but no tension, the second the converse. However, a non-engineer is less likely to comprehend the effect these differences can have on the stability of structures, their behaviour under alternating loads, the way they will fail or even collapse, the accuracy of predictions of their safety, and so on. Finally, and sadly, the subtleties of prestressed structures are also likely to remain something of a mystery to the non-engineer.

There is also the important matter of detail. Basic conceptions of structural behaviour (truss, beam, arch, etc.) are one thing, but most problems tend to arise at the level of detail – often minute detail. A cable is one of the easiest structures to conceive, but making it work – in terms of achieving the required strength, stiffness and bending properties, having suitable dynamic behaviour, corrosion, creep and fatigue characteristics, and manufacturing it to precisely the right length and fixing the ends – is a complex matter

efficiency. Another feature they share is that they can all be defined using relatively simple mathematical equations. This is essential if the engineer is to be able to build the mathematical model which will be needed to try to predict their structural behaviour. Many natural structures find their own form and do not fall into this category – spiders' webs, soap-film bubbles, taut nets. While small versions of such forms are easy to make, it has only recently become possible to create large-scale versions for use in buildings. In the late 1950s Frei Otto began developing various ways of scaling-up data gathered from small hanging models, but the real leap forward came when computers became powerful and quick enough to simulate the natural process of letting a structure find its own form.

Without a reasonable knowledge of the mathematical models used to represent loads, materials and structures, only a limited understanding of structures and their behaviour is possible. It

which few architects can, or need to, understand. The same is true of fabric and shell structures, the precise shape of which are sometimes believed to be a matter of relatively free choice.

It is thus inevitable that an architect, largely unaware of many of these complexities, will make choices which sometimes do not make for easy and cost-effective structural solutions. Perhaps most serious are the problems they can inadvertently cause by not understanding the significance of such secondary effects as stress concentrations and eccentrically applied loads which can make a structure prone to torsional instability.

There is, perhaps, a third position to defend, intermediate between what has been characterised as the engineering way of seeing structures and that of the architect, who sees them purely for their geometric, spatial, enclosing and iconographic functions. There are architects who incorporate the structure of a building into the architecture in more than a merely functional way. Derek

Sugden has made the 'irreverent but not necessarily irrelevant' observation that, between architectural form and engineering structure, there is 'archi-structure' – summarised, perhaps, as the architect's idea of what a functional structure of a building ought to look like. As with all ideas, it can be executed both well and poorly, and this book contains many examples of the former. But the phenomenon is hardly new: the ribs of late Gothic vaults do not carry loads in the same way as their early Gothic ancestors did; in the later fan vault, the ribs have virtually become appliqué.

What, then, do engineers see when they imagine or look at a structure? Broadly, they see patterns of loads which the structure must withstand; and they see load paths which conduct these loads through the structure to the foundations and the earth. The idea of the load path is very powerful, but it is perhaps a more nebulous concept than non-engineers might imagine. Sketches of load paths usually show lines and arrows, yet nothing actually flows. (A theoretician would say that it is, in fact, momentum which flows along a load path, but that's a bit obscure and doesn't help us here.) Also, the structure may be transmitting the load at one point along the load path by working in bending, at another by working in shear and at another by working in compression. Furthermore, in a finished building it is virtually impossible to affirm that loads actually are being carried along certain paths rather than others; and it may not even be certain that a structure is carrying these loads by means of one combination of structural actions rather than another. This is especially true of old buildings which will not now be working in precisely the way they were conceived to work by

ure of just one component or to progressive collapse. They see the behaviour of each element and sub-assembly in isolation, and of the entire structure as a whole. They see parts of the structure which might give rise to difficulties – insufficient or too much stiffness, and stress concentrations and instability (especially the inadequate bracing of frames and thin sheets of material required to carry compression).

Engineers see structures not as static objects but as things that move, and in various ways – deflection due to loads; movement caused by thermal expansion, foundation settlement and creep; movement at joints, which must be prevented, permitted, or allowed with some restraint in twelve possible degrees of freedom; movement in vibrations at the structure's natural frequency; and movement associated with the tolerances on component dimensions to allow them to be assembled yet be neither too loose nor too tight.

Structural engineers see the potential for materials to corrode or otherwise degrade, and to cause problems when they expand in warm weather or lose vital structural properties in a fire. They will also see a structure as having properties which impinge on the building envelope, the internal environment and the professional domains of the services engineer – thermal mass, U-values, sound absorption and so on. Finally, the structural engineer will see a structure as something that has to be built easily, cheaply, and quickly, and in a manner which is stable and safe at all times during construction.

Looking at a structure is an active process, even at the level of

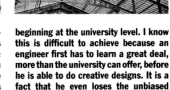

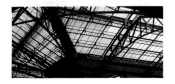

There is certainly no rule or recipe leading to good form, but there are means and ways towards it. The engineer, if he is interested, can contribute to it with variety and lightness. We must evoke the structural engineer's interest in this most inspiring part of his profession, beginning at the university level. I know this is difficult to achieve because an engineer first has to learn a great deal, more than the university can offer, before he is able to do creative designs. It is a fact that he even loses the unbiased approach to form and shape with which he enters the university. After some time, he will only design what he is able to analyse, which is not very much. The university must bring him over this hurdle.

Jörg Schlaich

the original designer (and may never have done so) – structural surveys depend heavily on experience and judgement. What can be said with complete confidence is that, if a building is standing, there will be a satisfactory series of load paths. If the building has survived other types of load during its life, such as heavy machinery or a hurricane, then it is also certain that, at that time, there must have been satisfactory loads paths for those loads too, though this may no longer be the case. These matters become of great concern as soon as someone proposes disturbing or removing parts of a building to effect repairs or adapt it to a new use and meet modern regulations.

As well as different structural actions along the various load paths, engineers can imagine the structure's likely behaviour under various loads – changing levels of stress, deflections and, for each combination of loads, likely collapse mechanisms. They see the inherent lack of safety in a structure which is vulnerable to the fail-

the words we use. In describing structures we need to categorise them. Engineers are likely to do this according to how they work, or think they work. Structures can be grouped into families or types, for instance, when we decide which word to use to describe them. This process of classification, or taxonomy as the biologists call it, is not necessarily objective; what one engineer sees as a truss, another might see as a beam with holes in (a perforated beam model was used when the Warren truss was first analysed in 1851). In general, engineers tend to categorise structures according to which mathematical model and technique of structural analysis they might use, although even this approach is becoming confused by computer programs which look only at local stresses and have a flagrant disregard for the principles of structure.

The following classification represents one perspective on structure; readers may have, or can develop, another for their own purposes.

Basic structural actions

	1-dimension	2-dimension	3-dimension
Compression	column strut wall	buttress flying buttress arch barrel vault	ribbed vault fan vault dome thin shells grid shells
Tension	tie cable hanger	catenary suspension bridge	shear-free (bubbles, cable nets) shear-resistant (fabrics, membranes)
Truss	n/a	statically determinate (pin-jointed, Warren truss, etc) statically indeterminate (redundant members, rigid joints, etc)	space truss lattice truss
Bending	beams one-way slab portal frames Vierendeel	grillage two-way slabs (flat, ribbed, coffered, etc.)	frames Kubik 'truss'
Shear	plate action shear wall	plate action shear wall	folded plates torsion

Complex structural actions

Combinations	post and lintel, column and beam, tied arch, jack arch
Composite materials	grp, grc, fibreglass, plywood, chipboard, etc.
Composite action	reinforced concrete; steel beam, metal decking with shear studs; concrete-encased steel column with shear studs
Stiffening	self weight (for arch or cantenary) trussing (for beam, arch or strut) truss action (for arch or catenary) beam action (for arch or catenary) folded plate action (for flat plate or thin shell)
Stabilising	geometry (bricks and voussoirs in walls, masonry arches, domes, etc.) tie downs (for masts, etc.) pre-stressing (self weight in gravity structures, tension and compression in strut and tie structures, tension in membranes)
Bracing	by triangulation by cross bracing or K-bracing (for frames) by portal action, rigid joints, Vierendeel action (for frames) by shear action (shear walls and plate action in floors)

Structural design

Good design is invisible for several reasons. People generally see only the finished product of the design process and a certain expertise is needed to infer the design effort that went into creating it. People also tend to notice and complain about bad design far more than they notice or praise good design. Furthermore, it is seldom possible to associate designs with individuals: engineering design is the result of collaboration between many members of a design team. Designs may not even have their origins with the current design team since much design is cumulative – once developed, ideas can be freely used by others and improved upon. The humble I-beam, for instance, is a brilliant piece of engineering design which enables buildings to be built using a fraction of the material which would otherwise be needed. Its development, and that of a thousand other structural devices, represents the cumulative effort and experience of many thousands of skilful engineers stretching back over many decades, even centuries.

It is also important to distinguish between two approaches to structural design representing different attitudes of mind. One way is to design structures by making imaginative use of existing bodies of engineering knowledge and relatively tried-and-tested structural solutions. The results, needless to say, are not likely to be highly innovative but may nevertheless suit a particular building project. Much architecture follows the same approach.

But many designers – both engineers and architects – believe that the best way to achieve good buildings is to go back to first principles and create designs by a combination of inspiration and logic. While architects are usually educated to take this approach, even to the extent of challenging a project brief by questioning the need for a building at all, it is not common in the formation of engineering students. Yet it is only in a climate where precedent and established practice are challenged and building design briefs do not continue to direct designers along well-trodden paths, that genuine innovation can be achieved. Then engineers can be at their most creative and achieve what, with hindsight, is called progress. Although this approach requires and stimulates skills that projects using standard design solutions seldom challenge, it also stems from an attitude of mind in the engineer – when asked how it happened that he was continuously asked to work on interesting projects, Peter Rice replied simply that many of them had not been very interesting when he was first approached.

The art of design, like many skills such as riding a bike or swimming, is learnt mainly by doing, not from reading descriptions of how it is done. Nevertheless, there can be benefit in trying to articulate what one is doing, for instance, by telling someone else. And when doing this, it is probably always the speaker who benefits more than the listener. Articulating what one is doing is a valuable way of raising one's own self awareness, and in this lies the road to improvement and the building of self esteem. In this light, it is interesting to wonder why architects ten to talk about their design process more than structural engineers. The diagram (right) shows how one engineer (Frank Newby) has expressed his view of the engineering design process.

Choosing and developing a structural concept for a particular purpose is a highly creative process. For an architect the form of the structure is constrained only by its function, the site and his or her vision. For structural engineers the form is also constrained by how they intend and expect it will work as a structure, and by the need to provide a rational argument and calculations to justify this

Architect's brief
– client and planning requirements
– flexibility of space and loading
– life of building
– allowable building time and costs
– proposed mechanical services, etc.
– architect's concept of the building

Structural climate
– availability and quality of materials
– availability and quality of workmanship
– ground conditions
– weather conditions
– local building regulation

Initial design process

Proposed structural schemes

Integration process — Feedback

Developed scheme

Confirmation process — Feedback

Detailed drawings Contract documents

Erection of building — Feedback

Store of information
– properties of materials
– deformation and stress characteristics of structural systems and foundations
– capabilities of structural analysis
– methods of manufacture and erection of structural components
– new developments and trends in the building industry
– experience of the integration of structures in architecture
– costs of construction

The foundation of engineering is knowledge of material, not, as engineers are so often apt to preach, a knowledge of mathematics.

Alan Harris

expectation before the structure is built. Considerable powers of imagination are needed. To design a structure it is necessary to imagine every conceivable type of failure and then ensure that each one is prevented by deft use of materials. To do this an engineer must be able to apply imaginary loads to structures that do not yet exist and which, even when built, will respond in ways which are too small or slow to see or, in the case of collapse, which he hopes never to see.

The initial choice of a structural scheme is made from a relatively limited number of basic structural forms or actions. These can be developed and adapted and used in combination with each other to create a unique and original whole. By and large, this will arise out of the nature of the loads which need to be carried and how they might be conducted along load paths to available points of support. The engineer's skill lies in choosing an arrangement which manages to satisfy, to varying degrees, many, often incompatible,

constraints. As with architecture and composing music, this skill relies on a mixture of precedent, experience and inspiration. Just how a particular engineer actually conceives a new structure is both highly individual and virtually impossible for anyone else to talk about.

Usually many different schemes will arise and their merits will be compared (qualitatively) with one another and according to how they each meet the functional, architectural, services and foundation requirements. Each scheme must then be tested by imagining how it will behave as a structure under the various loads. It may even be useful to make a string-and-sealing wax model, though more to assist the imagination than to glean any useful structural information. The real testing only begins at the next stage when the leap is made to a quantitative assessment of the structure.

Before the engineer can do any calculations to test a structural idea, a mathematical model of the whole structural system must be created. This model is a combination of three separate and entirely independent primary models – a model of the loads, a model of the material(s) and a model of the structure. The composite model becomes a set of relationships between the various elements of the three primary models – rather like the empty shell of a computer spreadsheet – into which particular values can be entered and certain results calculated. In this way the model can be made to behave and its response studied for a range of stimuli.

It must never be forgotten, however, that the primary models of loads, materials and structure are all idealisations and simplifications of the real world, and the behavioral output of the composite model is merely an infallible consequence of the information contained in the primary models, not of their real-world counterparts. Any predictions made from the output of the composite model about the likely behaviour of the completed structure must be treated with intelligence and care. There is risk associated with this inductive logic. On occasions, an experienced engineer may feel the risk is so great that confirmation of a different kind is advisable. Wind-tunnel tests and the building and testing of prototypes or accurate scale models can give valuable quantitative information about loads, stresses and deflections of structures. These will complement and may confirm the predictions made from purely theoretical 'tests'. Nevertheless, even such physical tests rely on various theories of engineering science for their interpretation and application to the full-size real structure. They, too, must therefore be used with great caution.

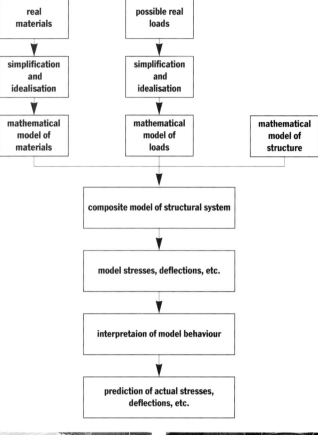

Any project has its cost constraints which must be met. They are a fundamental part of the design challenge, and finding a way to add one's special extra quality while respecting all the other parameters is one of the things which can make the challenge of design interesting and exciting to the engineer.

Peter Rice

Whatever type of structure is conceived, two important goals must be constantly borne in mind. Firstly, the structure must have a form and construction which can be described and specified in minute and precise detail, in order that it can be built. This is not always straightforward for concrete shells and fabric and cable-net structures. The geometrical capabilities of modern three-dimensional CAD software have enabled structures of unprecedented complexity to be built, partly for the simple reason that it is now possible to calculate their shapes and dimensions with greater ease and accuracy.

The computer has also helped structural engineers in meeting the other goal – providing a justification that a structure will perform as expected and be as safe as necessary. The sophisticated geometric computer models of complex structures form an essential part of the composite mathematical model needed to analyse a building's structural behaviour. This increased power to analyse a

broader range of structural forms and complexity of structure has brought enormous progress in recent years. Only twenty years ago many of the structures featured in this book – the fabric roofs, cable-net structures and highly redundant moment-resisting frames, to name just three – could not have been built because the mathematics of the geometry and the analysis would have been far too laborious to contemplate, even using the computers of that time. The requirement that a proposed structural form must be able to be justified is now far less restricting than it once was, although a negative consequence of this so-called progress is that it is now easier to produce inelegant and unnecessarily convoluted structures.

In this context it is vital to remember that the performance of a structure is entirely within the control of a good designer. The behaviour of a moment frame, truss or cable-net can be tuned as sensitively as any violin – by adjusting material specification, the type, size and cross-section of members, the position and rigidity of joints, the level of any prestressing, the attachment to any cladding with which it might act compositely, the effect of out-of-plane links such as longitudinal bracing, and so on.

All these technical aspects of the structural engineer's art are tools to be used at the appropriate time. They lie almost dormant in the back of the engineer's mind while he or she gets on with the more public, qualitative parts of the process. In dialogue with non-engineers the talk is of the location of columns, the size, shape and position of voids for services ducts and cables, the depth of floor structures, the location of shear cores, and the movement of different parts of the building relative to each other and the envelope (due to loads, settlement of foundations or thermal effects).

Each of these facets of a structure is interrelated, and the structural engineer is the person who understands their relationship. Take, for instance, the factors which affect the column grid in a building. The loads carried by individual columns need to be matched to the type and cost of different foundations, and these, in turn, depend on the load-carrying capacity of the soil. The column loads depend on the floor loading and the spans between columns which, in turn, affect the depth and spacing of the floor beams and, hence, the space for services, the height of the building and the cost of the cladding. In addition to these structural issues, there is also the influence of the various non-structural grids – the building envelope, the services distribution, furniture, room and corridor layout, basement car parks, and so on.

The advice given by an engineer concerning some area of his

between the rise of an arch and its stability and outward thrust. In a way which is half visual, half feeling, an engineer can imagine all the different consequences of changing column spacing, floor structure, a material, or the relative dimensions of members. The impression is of an imaginary object that is almost alive, much in the way that drivers of steam trains and old cars feel that their machines have their own character and behaviour. Rudyard Kipling wrote a wonderful story, 'The Ship That Found Herself' (not himself, note!), in which he brings alive the structure and engines of a transatlantic ship as they tell their experiences during a stormy voyage. It should be compulsory reading for every engineering degree.

These, then, are the essential aspects of the art of structural engineering design. Put another way, the structural engineer is someone who can make something with a tonne of material that 'any damn fool' can make with ten; someone who can make at full scale what anyone can make at a scale of 1:100 or 1:10; someone who can make for £100 what anyone can make for £1000. The Institution of Structural Engineers expresses the same idea rather more eloquently: 'structural engineering is the science of designing and making, with economy and elegance, buildings, bridges, frameworks, and other similar structures so that they can safely resist the forces to which they may be subjected.'

Much of this type of engineering knowledge cannot be written down and cannot be learnt quickly; it has to be built up gradually and through direct personal experience. It is small wonder that it takes many years to establish creative confident engineering teams

knowledge and skill might sometimes seem conveniently short and simple: 'Choose the form of a truss such that long members act in tension and short ones in compression'; or, 'For an efficient structure use tension in preference to compression, and either in preference to bending.' However, such simple rules are riddled with caveats (which is why engineers need fear nothing from so-called expert-systems). In the case of the truss, for instance, it depends on what uplift there may be, what restraint there is at the supports, whether you want a member to 'disappear' as the force within it goes from tension to compression, what materials and forms of those materials are available, and how much they cost.

The model of a universal building built up by the human mind is far too subtle to feed into any computer, and the workings of this mental image are far too fast to see. An engineer simply knows – feels – the nature of the relationship between floor span and depth, between the shape of a structural section and its deflection,

whose collective knowledge, skills and experience constitute a sufficient palette from which to conceive, evaluate and build new structures.

Engineer and architect

There often arises the question, 'Who designed that building?' The answer is usually, 'An architect.' Nearly always the truth is that a team of architects and engineers designed it. Yet the popular press and even well-known architectural periodicals consistently omit all mention of structural engineers, despite the occasional polite letter pointing the matter out.

Since the Copyright, Design and Patents Act of 1988, architect and structural engineer are treated equally in law. They each have the moral right – *le droit moral* – as co-author and copyright-owner of the design, to fix their name to a building they have designed. This law also gives both architect and engineer the right to have their name against any published photograph of the building. Furthermore, they also have the right to insist that their work is not subject to 'unjustified modification'. While this will not prevent building owners from making alterations, it does entitle architects and engineers to object to photographs of the altered artefacts being published; and they can have their identification removed from the building if they feel it has been degraded by a later hand.

Despite equality in law, the relationship between structural engineer and architect is not symmetrical. Maybe this is why so much has been written about the relationship. The nature of the responsibility each carries is different. If a building is an architectural failure, reputations and bank accounts may suffer; if it experiences a services failure people get too cold or hot. A structural engineer needs to have the confidence to sign a piece of paper saying 'this building will stand up safely for a long time'; he needs all the help he can get to achieve this level of confidence.

Perhaps the relationship fascinates so many writers because the modern architect is utterly dependent on the structural engineer. Yet engineers frequently feel equally dependent on the architect, from whom they may, or may not, get their next job.

There is also the question of authorship, and this can be a very sensitive issue. Human relationships occur in threes rather than twos; it is client, architect, engineer, not just the last two. And in groups of three, jealousies can arise. For example, architects will clearly want to protect their relationship with the client. Yet, is this reason enough for many architects, even some well-known for their structural architecture, to write and talk about buildings as if

successful design collaboration than there are recipes for a successful marriage.

Looking at all this another way, engineers have skills which architects lack, and *vice versa*. A sensible architect would surely want to collaborate on the creation of a building which exhibits evidence of more than the sum of two separate sets of skills. But there is always a difficulty when two people with different skills work together. Anyone who has tried to brief a lawyer will know the problem: 'Why didn't you tell me that before?' 'You didn't ask me?' 'How could I ask you if I didn't know what to ask?' 'You should know more about the law.' 'But that's why I'm employing you.' … and so on.

Some people suggest the solution to the gap and discord between the two professions is for them to study together. Others believe that a separation is essential since the very best architecture results from the interaction of unlike minds and creative tensions. Nevertheless, both groups would probably agree that, for the best results, it is beneficial for each profession to know what might be expected of the other, even if this is ignored. It would also be wise to expose and avoid genuine misunderstandings – all engineers and architects should read Alan Harris's *Architectural Misconceptions of Engineering*. Many engineers' lives are made miserable by architects who do not realise the consequences of some of their choices and decisions, or are not even aware that they ought to consider the consequences. Conversely, it is not uncommon for engineers to feel that they are seldom challenged enough by architects, being asked merely to make a building work structurally after most of

Where structure is a major consideration, the engineer should be a partner in evolving the design, so that the proper integration of structure and architecture can be achieved. It is of course his job to assist the architect to realise his architectural conception, and he must accept his role as an assistant. But he should be a useful assistant, and that means that he must understand and sympathise with the aims of the architect, so that he, in his own intuitive thinking, can arrive at proposals which will further the architect's wishes – just as a pianist in his own right should not deem it beneath his dignity to act as an accompanist, as long as he is not asked to play with one finger.

Ove Arup

the design team contained no structural engineers? Conversely, one prominent engineer declined the opportunity to be credited as co-designer of a building for fear that his architect collaborators might feel he was trying to steal their glory and so would not want to work with him in the future. Does it all come down to the fact that engineers are numerate and architects are visual? If so, why? The roots to such attitudes and emotions go very deep and it all gets very psychological, very quickly.

Like most team activities, the circumstances and type of undertaking influence the nature of the collaboration. In a major civil engineering project the engineer's contribution is dominant; in a bespoke private residence, the architect is to the fore. In hospitals, sports stadia and theatres the contribution is more evenly shared. Personalities, too, are important. There are as many different types of architect/engineer relationships as there are types of married couple. Likewise, there are no more guidelines for a

the design is complete. Although this is one of their vital skills, engineers have many others, including the ability to:
- bring experience from other projects (an engineer will work on many more projects than an architect);
- suggest appropriate structural forms;
- imagine the likely behaviour of a structure that does not yet exist;
- think both qualitatively and quantitatively about loads, materials and structures and switch between both modes of thought;
- have a feel for the properties and behaviour of materials;
- devise a design procedure for a type of structure that has never before been designed or built;
- build scale models to test structural ideas and behaviour and interpret, for use at full size, the results

obtained from a scale model;

- choose appropriate performance criteria against which a structure can be assessed, and limits which it must not transgress;
- understand the implications for other professionals (concerning cost, services, durability, fire resistance, etc.) of the building structure, and *vice versa*;
- assess the buildability of a proposed design and suggest how it can be improved;
- know when the process of structural design has been completed in a satisfactory manner;
- fall back on 'engineering judgement' when all else fails.

The role of both engineers and architects is currently under threat. Some of their work is being taken over by others – quantity surveyors, project managers, design-and-build firms and specialist contractors. Part of the reason for this is that architects and engineers have become too specialised and others have begun, more and more, to manage projects, deal with clients, estimate and control costs, and design for production. On the other hand, they have perhaps done too little to make known the full range of their skills and their place in the process of designing and making a building. One reason why competitive fee tendering has had such a savage effect on both professions is that clients have been unable to understand what it is that engineers and architects contribute that they cannot get, for instance, from a design-and-build firm or a con-

offering needs to be marketed far more effectively than has been necessary in the past. This means articulating the design process and getting people to understand how difficult and time consuming it can be; in short, overcoming the inherent invisibility of what is largely an intellectual process.

Structure and aesthetics

I start from the premise that to be a good structural engineer it is essential to be able to discriminate between good and bad examples of structural engineering. Concern with aesthetics should be addressing what constitutes good and bad design and what it is to be a good structural engineer.

This approach to aesthetics – the study of excellence in an area of creative human activity – is far broader than that of the classical Greek philosophers who studied only what can be directly perceived by the five senses. Nowadays we can no longer keep separate the stimuli from the senses and their interpretation in our minds. The aesthetics of structure go far deeper than how something looks – much depends on who is doing the looking.

The outcome of considering the aesthetics of structure should not be a precise set of rules for creating a good structure. Rather, it should be a better-developed ability to discriminate between good and bad engineering, and a stronger sense that good engineering design matters and can bring a wealth of benefits to building owners, architects and architecture – and to engineers themselves, both personally and collectively as a profession.

The underlying principles of aesthetics can apply equally well to

What happens when one works with different architects is that each architect's attitudes and opinions become part of the problem being solved. And provided one can introduce – as one almost invariably can – an element of engineering exploration either in the nature of materials, or structure, or light, or some other physical phenomenon, no loss of identity or independence need be implied for the engineer.

Peter Rice

Artistic quality or 'delight' can be compared to a coy maiden who will shrink from direct pursuit but pretend to ignore her and get on with your work and she may come running after you. My advice to engineers is to be good engineers first of all.

Ove Arup

tractor. The result, at the time of writing, is that engineers and architects are working long hours. At a time when designers are being urged to take on more and more – energy conservation, green issues, production engineering matters, maintainability – they are being given less time and money to do so.

The consequences are inevitable: if key structural issues are not dealt with early in a project they will need to be done later, and will cost more. The following story is true. On a project which needed a large and complex façade structure, bids were accepted for the cladding and the building structure. Only later did the cladding contractor realise the complexity of the structural issues involved and the client had to employ a second firm of structural engineers, at more expense, to resolve matters. As more examples come to light, perhaps more clients will realise that you only get what you pay for, and the earlier in the project you do it, the cheaper it is.

The lesson for all building designers is clear – the service they are

any work – functional objects such as a tin-opener, 'useless' objects such as paintings, or objects lying somewhere in between, such as an attractive table lamp or a roof structure. Discussion focuses on the various criteria according to which the work might be judged, and the relative importance of these criteria.

Exactly who is offering their views on a work of art is significant. A modern engineer looking at a Gothic cathedral (and its load paths, equilibrium of thrusts, wind bracing, etc.) is seeing a different building from an architect, sculptor or, indeed, a medieval master mason. Perceiving or looking at a structure, either as engineer, architect or sculptor, depends on a knowledge of cultural context and precedent as well as on education and skills of interpretation.

Most of us could quickly list the qualities of a good tin-opener; it would be more challenging to do the same for a painting, or roof structure. Discerning quality in a work of art is often wrapped up in the activity of criticism. The quality of a Rembrandt, a Wren church, or a Rover car arises, in part, from what people say about it, who is saying it, how they make their case for its excellence, and how successful they are at persuading others of their view. It is thus vital to the existence and success of any creative art that there is regular debate – not only so that existing works may be evaluated, but also so that a culture of excellence and quality surrounding that particular art can develop.

An immediate outcome for someone considering the aesthetics of their art will be an improved ability to identify appropriate criteria for judging excellence, to formulate powerful arguments using good rhetoric as to why a particular work is a good one and to criticise an existing work, perhaps even one of their own design or making. In the longer term, the outcome will be better designs and artefacts.

Whatever the reason, it is a fact that there is very much more debate about the aesthetics of architecture than of structural engineering. And yet good engineers do have a well-developed sense of excellence in their art. There are perhaps good psychological reasons why the education and training of engineers does not generally involve the 'crits' so beloved of architecture schools. Engineers are generally brought up on a diet of correct (or incorrect) answers to specified problems – not much room there for debate. Even in open-ended projects there often tends to be an underlying idea that proposals are either right or wrong, rather than having different good and bad points.

A work of art communicates with whoever is experiencing it. Most creators of works of art intend to communicate something,

ture. It will reflect the cultural and engineering climate in which it was conceived and realised. It may communicate some eternal truths or laws of nature: truths about equilibrium and statics, about the nature of structure, or about the mechanical properties of materials. A structure will tell us something of a culture's manufacturing technologies, of the properties of materials which dictate how they may, or may not, be manufactured. It may convey the full wealth of a material's *aesthetic*, its soul. Above all, it will communicate the skill of the designer and the manufacturer.

Good structures are often praised for their elegance. This may well be a reflection of how they look, but when engineers talk of elegant design they mean rather more. There is the hint of an artefact that makes the job it does look easy. Often you can only read this in a design if you know how hard the job was. Engineers allude to this in their claim that 'if a design looks right, it is right', which sounds arrogant but is seldom meant so. Take, for instance, a problem encountered in many roof structures – joining perhaps a dozen members together at one connection. Some designs make this task look easy; others evoke sympathy for the craftsmen who had to fashion and assemble them, even for the materials, bolts and gusset plates themselves!

Engineering elegance is manifest also in the subtlety of the engineering principles employed. The use of post-tensioning, for instance, might substantially reduce the amount of material needed to make a floor structure, with little cost penalty and the bonus of an additional storey squeezed into a building. By exploiting the ductile strength of steel, a new means of safeguarding

If the structural shape does not correspond to the materials of which it is made there can be no aesthetic satisfaction ... Our capacity to develop the aesthetic quality of structural harmony, in terms of different materials and its structural requirements, is as undeveloped in our time as orchestration and counterpoint were in the seventeenth century. The reason is possibly the spiritual divorce of our specialised techniques.

Eduardo Torroja

something from within themselves. People talk of works of art 'speaking for themselves', perhaps on behalf their creators. Engineers talk of 'reading a structure'. But the act of communication only works if we understand the language of communication; and the power and effectiveness of the communication depends on the quality of its rhetoric. All this happens when we look at a structure, and in making a judgement about it we are, in effect, answering the question, 'What does this structure say to me?'

At the level of sensations, we perceive the size, form, mass, scale, texture and colour of a structure; and we tend to interpret these in ways are influenced by our culture – as proportion, simplicity, delicacy, elegance. But, most of all, we react to structures. They evoke eye movement; they elicit exclamations of admiration, or otherwise; they rouse enthusiasms such as the desire to look at or take photographs of them, return for second visits, and so on.

A structure may remind us of something in our history or cul-

against collapse in an earthquake zone might be devised which uses less material and releases valuable space for windows and useful floor area.

Materials might be used elegantly in combination to derive benefit from different properties. The strength in tension of glass fibre, and the mass, strength in compression and low cost of cement can be combined in glass-reinforced cement to give a material capable of high resistance to bending and intricate mouldability. By welding shear studs to a steel column and encasing the whole in concrete, the two materials achieve composite action, combining the benefits of steel's strength, stiffness and ease of connection, with the compressive strength, mass, mouldability and fire resistance of concrete.

The structural engineer is constantly seeking, and finding, ever more elegant ways of manufacturing buildings and their components – using standard products to create bespoke designs; devising a structural system which can be made up in factory conditions as a kit of parts for rapid erection on site; using ferrocemento moulds as permanent formwork for a concrete floor to give an exceptional finish to the soffit.

Another aspect of a structure's elegance is the way in which it can simultaneously achieve many functions with economy of components, material and cost. A particularly rich field is that of the interaction between structures and building services. A range of strategies is available, each of which can have its own elegance.

The designers might opt for total separation or zoning. With this method the likelihood of interference is minimised and later changes to the services, and even to the structure, are made easy. Alternatively, certain agreed spaces may be shared, perhaps by using natural voids, such as space between floor beams or holes in castellated beams and roof trusses. A further stage of integration is the planned interpenetration of services runs and structural elements such as dedicated holes and voids made especially for services. A much more efficient use of overall volume can thus be achieved, but with the penalty of the additional effort needed to achieve the co-ordination, and inflexibility in the future.

Finally there is the elegance of total integration achieved when structural components act as parts of the building services systems:
- a concrete plank may contain precast holes that serve as air ducts;
- beams or a floor structure may form the walls of an air duct;
- the thermal inertia of a structural element may be

ture. A complete list would, of course, verge on the tedious since it would need to include the visual arts and architecture as well as highly practical matters such as durability, serviceability and economy. The following is my list of some of the criteria I use when looking at, judging and designing structures; it goes a little further than 'firmness, commodity and delight'. Readers will have, or may develop, their own.
- the skill and clarity with which structural actions, such as tension, compression, bending and shell action, are used and expressed (or hidden);
- elegance and simplicity in joints, structural elements and the structure as a whole;
- structural honesty, or dishonesty when appropriate;
- expression of an appropriate degree of solidity or delicacy;
- economy of material and the appropriateness of a material to its structural function;
- awareness, exploitation and expression of each material's unique aesthetic;
- the choice of a design solution that succeeds in avoiding difficulties rather than surmounting them;
- expression of structural actions in joints;
- juxtaposition of the materials and functions of structural members at joints;
- expression, in a structure's geometry or form, of the imposed loads, structural actions and internal stresses;

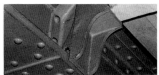

I believe we can rethink the way we can use many materials, especially how they are detailed, to express more clearly their engineering nature, and thereby find a new and interesting aesthetic.

Peter Rice

exploited to store heat or coolth;
- structure may absorb or reflect sound, or absorb vibrations of machinery;
- structure may conduct heat or electricity (or not) and allow light to penetrate (or not);
- part of a structure may be filled with water to provide active fire protection.

Likewise, services elements may have a structural function:
- a services core that is also a shear wall;
- a column or beam that also carries away rainwater;
- a duct that also carries loads (for example, those arising from self weight, expansion, wind).

From these examples we can begin to draw up a list of criteria by which we might judge the quality, excellence or elegance of a struc-

- expression of natural geometries such as the circle or catenary;
- selection of a structural form that sensibly anticipates the means by which it can be described (defined) and justified;
- allusion to structural precedents from history, other cultures or nature;
- degree of integration between load-bearing aspects of a structure and non-load-bearing aspects such as cladding and building services;
- expression of the structure's method of construction;
- devising of structural systems capable of repetitive manufacturing processes while retaining stimulating variation and irregularity;
- intelligent anticipation of production engineering problems at the design stage.

Criteria such as these can also help us develop our idea of progress in structural engineering, which is not as obvious as some people would like to believe – it has been observed that modern Codes of Practice are more tedious, no safer and lead to more expensive buildings. Is this progress? People seldom talk of what constitutes progress or how you might evaluate a change and establish whether it would take matters forward or backwards in time. It is a challenging and rewarding exercise to compare two structures built at different times and list all the reasons why one must have been built earlier than the other, or why they could not have been constructed in the other order.

There is surely something to be learnt from the processes of becoming an architect, musician or painter. Criticism and discussion of good and bad, and old and new exemplars of their art play a central part in their education. Surely the formation of structural engineers should include structural criticism, analogous to architectural or music criticism. It would improve their powers of analysis and understanding. It would enhance their ability to explain why a certain structure is well designed and another less well designed, why some deserve their status as classics, why Nervi, Owen Williams and Torroja were great structural engineers. It might also become easier for engineers to articulate to others the nature of structural engineering design as an activity, and thereby reduce the tendency of many to overlook it. Not least, it might also reduce the number of classic structures which are destroyed or molested beyond redemption through ignorance.

By this means, I suspect, engineers' self-esteem and status might

While these matters are both important and useful, focusing on them alone can, I believe, lead people to overlook the two most important issues in structural engineering – the building as a whole and the client who wants the building.

Although these appear to be two separate issues, it can be helpful to unite them by considering the single idea of *building performance* and addressing the building brief as a statement of the performance that the client requires of his building. This may not be clear at the beginning of a project, especially for a client who has only rarely commissioned a building. An important role for the design team is to develop the brief with the client until it becomes clear and sufficiently well defined for them to proceed in the right direction. This process requires an active input from the client. Unfortunately, many building projects go wrong because the design team does not get clear guidance or the appropriate input from the client or the project manager as the client's representative.

However, the idea of building performance can be misused – issuing a performance specification can be a way of avoiding doing the design work itself, and the specification itself can, of course, be wrong. Thus one designer can pass responsibility for design (or, rather, for bad design) onto another, perhaps a specialist, who may not be in a position to deliver it. When the building element finally is designed it can often fail to serve the purpose for which it was originally intended. Similarly, the performance of individual elements of a building can be carefully specified and accurately delivered, while the performance of the whole building may not be satisfactory. This usually results in huge legal costs and the client

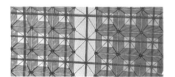

A technically perfect work can be aesthetically inexpressive but there does not exist, either in the past or the present, a work of architecture which is accepted and recognized as excellent from the aesthetic point of view which is not also excellent from the technical point of view. Good engineering seems to be a necessary though not sufficient condition for good architecture.

Pier Luigi Nervi

begin to rise towards the levels of a century ago; and both clients and architects would better understand the full variety and value of what engineers could contribute to their construction projects, and that it would be worth paying for.

The nature of structural engineering
Books about the engineering of buildings usually focus on the engineers' view of their subject and the bodies of knowledge which enable them to undertake their work. Some books are devoted to the properties of different materials and their respective codes of design practice. Others look at the different types and forms of structure such as beams, frames, trusses, membranes or shells, as well as the various ways of analysing the behaviour of such structures, while others consider various detailed construction issues such as the design of connections.

does not get his building on time or at the intended cost. In both these cases, although the client does not get what he wanted, there seems to be no-one to blame. In fact the cause is a failure to comprehend the totality of a building system and the error is committed at the very outset.

Problems such as these have, to a large extent, been solved in the aerospace and car industries during the last thirty years. In these industries the whole artefact is now considered as a series of interacting engineering systems – the fuel system, the cooling system, the transmission system, and so on. In this manner the performance of each whole system is considered, as well as the integration of the various systems. In the building industry, however, it is still usual to divide things up according to the ancient professional disciplines. Thus responsibility for the horizontal load-bearing system changes between the structural engineer and the façade engineer at the point where they are connected. This frequently leads to misunderstandings of the overall performance. Similar problems can arise when the thermal properties of structural or façade components of a building have a significant influence on the thermal performance of an entire building.

Now that clients are demanding that buildings perform more and more efficiently, it will be essential to approach their design in terms of the major engineering systems. When one car manufacturer changed to this systems approach to design, they were able to achieve a 20 per cent increase in the efficiency of the entire transmission system, from the engine through to the road. There is no reason why this approach could not deliver similar improvements in building engineering. Innovative engineering firms will be able to offer their clients buildings that perform very much more efficiently than those of today.

Taking into account the needs of the client is, of course, not a new idea. However, all construction professionals – engineers, architects, quantity surveyors – are torn between the need to serve the client and to earn sufficient income. It is a brave architect who persuades the client he does not need a building. But in this example we do have a view of the future. Structural engineers have traditionally earned their fees by providing a safe steel or concrete structure to support the envelope and people inside. Likewise services engineers have earned fees providing boilers, ducts and pumps. Actually, clients never want these – they want the space and internal environment necessary to undertake their business, and this may be achieved without a traditional structure or heating and ventilation. To meet these needs all building engineers will need to

a different building. Engineers have much to learn from architects about how to persuade clients they have something worthwhile to bring to a project. Unless engineers learn fast their position and their fees will be taken by contractors and they will be consigned to the role of calculators and code checkers.

The fifty or so buildings presented in this book aim to show how engineers contribute to projects and deliver clients what they want. Indeed engineers can often deliver more than the client originally imagined. The projects have been grouped under six broad headings which reflect different ways that structural engineers can provide a service to their clients, over and above the minimum task of delivering pieces of steel, timber and concrete. They reflect the skills that engineers can bring to projects which no-one else can. The engineers' understanding of structural form, materials, construction methods and costs are merely the means by which they can provide the various aspects of what it is that clients want, or what architects may want on their client's behalf. The six chapter headings are:

– the process of engineering: design development;
– devising buildings that work for architect, client and occupier;
– creating value for the client;
– exploring the unknown: managing risk and delivering confidence;
– putting structure on show: the engineering aesthetic of materials;
– realising dreams.

The basis of engineering is knowledge of the materials being used: knowledge of what they are made of, how they are made, how they are shaped, how you fit them together, how they stand up to stress, how they break, how they catch fire, how they react to all the various agencies of ruin which are perpetually nibbling at them, how in due course all fall down.

Alan Harris

find new ways of earning their living apart from their traditional role sizing components and equipment. Few engineers are yet facing up to this challenge. Perhaps the best examples are among building services engineers who earn fees by persuading clients they do not need tonnes of equipment to heat and condition their buildings when natural ventilation, with little equipment, can meet the client's needs.

Although marketing is not the main theme of this book, I believe engineers nowadays need to articulate more effectively what they do in order to persuade clients to employ them. It is not at all obvious to many clients just what consulting engineers do and what contribution they might make to a project. In the absence of such marketing many clients are persuaded by contractors that consulting engineers are an unnecessary luxury. This may be true for undemanding projects, just as it is possible to design and build a house without employing an architect. However, the result will be

In fact, all projects involve each strand of the structural engineer's art to some degree. The projects have not been placed in a certain chapter because they involve only that aspect of engineering; rather they have been so placed because they happen to illustrate a certain aspect more clearly than another project. Nor have the projects been selected because they are superlatives, the best of their kind in the world, or by the most famous engineers or architects. The work of good engineers is apparent to those who choose to look for it in projects large and small. In choosing these projects I have had to reject twenty times as many; there is a lot of good building engineering around these days. There is also a lot of bad. If nothing else, I hope this book helps people understand what good engineering is, and how to recognise it. By this means they will come to value it more highly.

The process of engineering: design development

When designing a building we begin with the client's brief and a blank sheet of paper. We see various architectural, structural and services design concepts appear, develop and, sometimes, disappear. We end with a building, designed in all its substantial details, and with all the major decisions made about how it will be fabricated and constructed.

It is seldom apparent in a finished building how it became the way it is, how the engineering solutions came about. What is virtually certain is that they came about through a process of evolution. Ideas are proposed and tested, sometimes using physical models, sometimes using mathematical models or, most often, simply in the minds of engineers. The tests can be against dozens of criteria – strength, stiffness, weight, economy, ease of construction, appearance, and so on. In the light of the evaluation, new ideas are proposed which are better in some way. And the process repeats, again and again, until the design process has to stop, limited by time or money.

Although they may not realise it, those who buy the services of design engineers are buying mainly their ability to be creative, to have ideas, criticise and evaluate them and to improve them – the very process of designing. This is not like buying a car. You know what the car is like and how it performs. When you buy an engineer's services you are buying the potential to create something that does not yet exist. Engineers often get appointed on the strength of ideas that have not yet been shown to work. Their skill as designers is to develop the ideas so that they do work. Sometimes an innovative idea turns out not capable of being made to work (within time or budget). The good engineer will have anticipated such 'failure' and devised, in parallel with the innovative idea, a more straight-forward alternative. But it is only the good engineer who tries the new idea in the first place, for only by trying new ideas does engineering progress.

The engineer's skill, then, is far more than a mere ability to calculate a stress or deflection. It is both complex and complicated – rich in structure and rich in detail. It comprises analytical, organisational and social skills. The engineering design process involves the interaction and integration of the structural engineer's contribution with those of other members of the design team – architects, services engineers, specialist contractors, quantity surveyors. Ideas for different elements of a design arise from many sources and for all sorts of reasons. Some groups of ideas will naturally develop together, feeding off one another; other ideas will be totally incompatible with one another. Some ideas might spark off trains of thought in entirely new directions. Even when the brief is a good one, it, too, is likely to change once design has begun.

Each group of designers will behave and interact during this process in their own unique way – there are no rules or methods to follow. Usually, some members of a design team will have worked together before and ideas from previous projects are likely to re-emerge. Ultimately it is only the idea of the goal that focuses the group's attention and activity, though early in a project this goal is seldom clearly defined.

So, in one manner or another, designs develop. Early on, many different possibilities will be considered; gradually ideas begin to interlock, at first loosely, then more firmly. Finally, the many different strands of the structural design and the architectural and services design, become so integrated and inter-related – so highly engineered – that it becomes virtually impossible to alter one feature without affecting many, perhaps all the others. It is for this reason that the idea of 'optimisation' is often so meaningless in building design. There are usually several stages during design development after which it is simply not cost-effective to go back and consider significantly different proposals. Ultimately, good design can only be achieved by employing good designers.

The buildings in this chapter illustrate different aspects of how engineers develop and improve designs from outline ideas to reality. The key to the success of Commerzbank was developing the means for constructing the tallest building in Frankfurt on a clay soil that is notoriously weak and inconsistent. A new type of foundation was devised and an entirely new type of structural steel frame was developed, creating a building that weighs less than half the weight of a concrete frame that would be usual in Germany. The same design team worked together on the Barcelona Communications Tower where a standard structural idea – the cable-stayed mast – was developed by the addition of trusses and the use of pre-stressing, into a radically new structural form of great elegance.

At the Inland Revenue Offices in Nottingham and the ITN headquarters, conventional methods of construction would have been too slow and costly. New methods were developed to remove the slow and labour-intensive activities from the critical path of the construction programme. The enormous castings at Ponds Forge, and the membrane canopy at the Don Valley Stadium, both in Sheffield, illustrate two different ways in which the form of structural elements can be developed. For the casting, the form is created by gradually reducing the amount of metal to the minimum that will carry the loads. The shape of the membrane canopy is found using software which iteratively modifies the form until it simultaneously satisfies conditions of statical equilibrium and the geometry of the boundary conditions.

The two glass roofs of the D.G. Bank and the Hippopotamus house in Berlin are part of a much longer development story which has fascinated engineers and architects since they were first used in botanical gardens in the 1840s, for example at Bicton in Devon and at the Kibble Palace in Glasgow. The challenge for the modern engineer has been to recreate the same elegance while adding something new, making them cost-effective in today's economic climate and ensuring they satisfy the much more stringent wind-loading required by modern codes of design practice.

Commerzbank

Frankfurt 1994–1997

Structural engineer Jack Zunz, Chris Wise, Harry Bridges, Peter Bailey, Chris Smith, Sean Walsh, Gabriele Del Mese – <u>Ove Arup & Partners</u>

The designers of the new headquarters building for the Commerzbank were selected on the basis of a limited Ideas Competition. Twelve practices were invited to enter, nine from Germany, two from the USA and Sir Norman Foster & Partners from Britain. Fosters chose to develop their entry with Ove Arup & Partners, largely on the basis of many previous successful collaborations. The brief was distributed on 13 February 1991 and competition entries had to be delivered by 3 June.

The brief and building context

From the first page of the brief it was clear that the client was seeking an unusual, indeed, an innovative building. After the three principal aims of the competition was the embracing requirement that 'die Verträglichkeit der Lösung mit der Umgebung hat gleichen Rang wie der Nutzwert' (the environmental friendliness of the design shall be as important as functional worth). The Commerzbank's mission statement gave other clues to its attitude to the built environment: 'The spirit of a company determines its architecture and its architecture reflects the image of a company'. And, more particularly: 'Wir engagieren uns für umweltverträglichen Fortschritt' (we are committed to environmentally-friendly progress). In this light the Bank was clear about the significance of the new building: 'Through the creation of an ecologically-sound building, we have the chance to portray ourselves as an innovative Bank which takes its social responsibility seriously.

With a building which will stand at the forefront of environmentally-friendly architecture for many years to come, we will display that aspect of the Bank's personality which favourably differentiates us from our competitors.'

Throughout the brief, internal and external environmental issues were mentioned again and again. Despite being a restricted site, there was a requirement to create new green space. There was encouragement to employ 'innovative concepts' and energy-saving systems for the mechanical services. Heating and lighting needs should be reduced, and natural ventilation should be used as much as possible. Even in the high-rise part of the development, fresh-air ventilation was required which could be achieved by opening windows, as long as safety and draught-free airflow was ensured. Similarly, the need for cooling should be reduced by giving adequate protection from the heat and light of the sun.

The building concept should aim to reduce the external envelope to a minimum for the given enclosed volume, achieve an energy-efficient disposition of enclosed volumes, exploit passive heat gain, avoid draughts, minimise disturbance of the ground water level and consider measures such as roof gardens to compensate for area of ground occupied by the building. Even in the construction process itself, the environment should be safeguarded: all construction should be energy saving, building materials and processes should be environmentally friendly, construction waste should be

avoided or recycled, and an energy-saving construction method should be used.

Adopting this broadly 'green' approach was also seen as bringing great commercial benefits by adding to the value of the site, improving the total cost-effectiveness of the building and, by reducing the running and maintenance costs, improving the rentability of the floor space.

Finally, among just four criteria on which the competition entries would be judged, was 'environmental friendliness/approach to energy issues'.

The brief, of course, contained all the more usual prescriptions: the floor area needed, the likely height (about 160 metres) and location of the main entrance, the allowable proximity to the Bank's existing 30-storey building on the same site (both above and below ground), the listed buildings that needed to be protected, and so on. One other matter that received particular mention was the requirement that core floor areas (<u>Kernflächen</u>) must not be concentrated centrally and could serve several floors so that 'a limited number of storeys can be openly linked together'.

Conception – the competition scheme

The response of designers to a brief is a mixture of many things: picking out key ideas from the brief, taking inspiration from the client, the cultural climate or specific aspects of the site and, of course, the designers' own experiences and enthusiasms, as well as ideas based on fundamental principles, clear logic and a consideration of the way materi-

Services Engineers   Dr Michael Schmidt, Klaus Bode, Ian
Mulquiney, Graham Cossons, John Perry
Roger Preston / Klimasystemtechnik
(RP+KSozietät)

Client   Commerzbank AG

als and structures work and can be manufactured.

The shape of the site and the proximity of the existing 30-storey tower clearly favoured a non-rectangular plan, and the idea that it should be triangular came very early. One proposal arose from the need to shield the office floors from solar gain. Common areas and

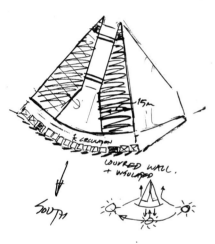

access ways could be on the south face of the building with the office space housed in two wedges. All three sections would be linked to work as a structurally efficient tube.

However, a study of the energy equations soon showed that the main source of heat gain was not the sun but electrical equipment within the building. A wider range of possible high-rise structures was then looked at, all based on a triangular plan and with different ways of achieving sufficient lateral and torsional stability, some in the form of a structural tube, others with a central core.

Inspired, perhaps, by the phrase in the brief about linking groups of floors

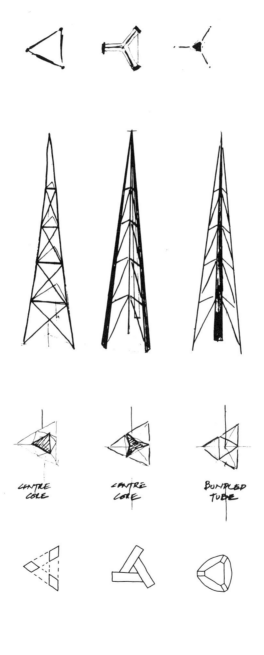

CENTRE CORE   CENTRE CORE   BUNDLED TUBE

together, and the suggestion to consider roof gardens, the idea arose of creating a perforated tube – groups of storeys alternating with garden spaces. A tube was favoured since it is inherently stiffer

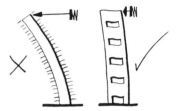

than a central-core scheme (the section has a larger second moment of area in plan).

The problem with such an idea, though, was how to make the structure stiff enough in the storeys with gardens. Cross-bracing would defeat the object of the voids and it would not be feasible to

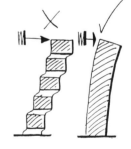

make the columns of a giant Vierendeel frame stiff enough. In a high-rise building the stiffness of the entire building and of each floor has to be carefully limited because of what engineers colloquially refer to as 'the P-delta effect'. If a column sways too far away from the vertical there comes a point when the vertical load (P) which it supports is shifted laterally (δ) to such a degree relative to the base that overturning due to the eccentric load overcomes the column's ability to restore itself to the vertical. To prevent such instability and

17

dramatic collapse, overall sway is limited about 1:500, and single-storey sway to about 1:700.

Then came the flash of inspiration. By having the garden void on just one side of the triangular building, and by rotating this plan up the building, each storey of the building would comprise one garden area and two office areas, and this would enable adequate lateral stiffness to be developed.

Groups of six storeys, which came to be known as villages, would alternate

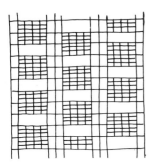

with three-storey-high, glass-walled voids which would enclose the garden areas. The structure of each village could be braced in the plane of the façade using Vierendeel action and serve to link the main vertical structure in the three perimeter towers. Within each village, the frame would reflect the higher bending moments and shear forces near the corner towers due to gravity loads. Towards the main columns, beams would be deeper, and columns wider and closer together. Out of all these structural considerations there was beginning to emerge a powerful architectural image for the visual appearance of the building.

Meanwhile, different ways of bracing

the structure were still being discussed, including tension cross-bracing, trusses and outrigger schemes. Some ideas contained hints of previous Foster/Arup collaborations, including the Hong Kong & Shanghai Bank and the Barcelona Communications Tower. Gradually the idea of using Vierendeel bracing was becoming more firmly established and attention focused on the cores and how they would discharge their several functions: primary load-bearing structure, lateral stability, vertical services distribution leading into horizontal distribution at each storey, vertical transportation and housing the communal areas on each floor.

In parallel with the development of the tower's superstructure, the means of providing it with suitable foundations

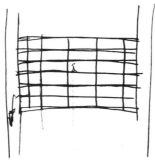

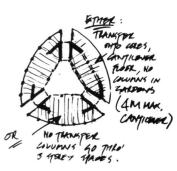

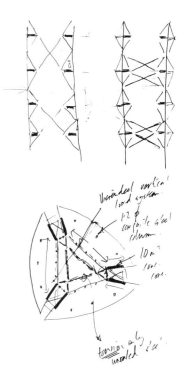

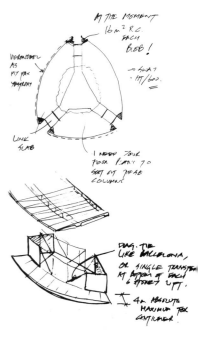

Architect   Spencer de Grey, Ken Shuttleworth, Mark Sutcliffe, John Silver, Tom Politowicz, Brandon Haw, Robin Partington, Paul Kalkhoven, Hans Brouwer, Uwe Nienstedt –

Sir Norman Foster & Partners

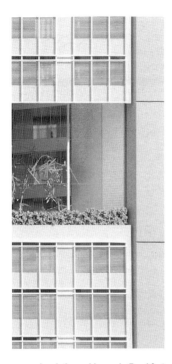

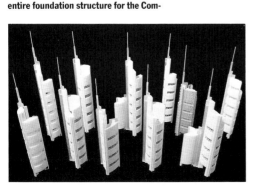

were also being addressed. Frankfurt sits on a bed of clay about 30 metres deep; below this is the Inflata layer which, although it has the characteristics of rock, is a highly irregular succession of limestone, calcerous sand and silt and the occasional layer of clay. It is also permeated by voids, some as large as 2 metres wide. Because of this variability, no building foundations in the city have ever penetrated into the Inflata layer and, consequently, there is no experience of working in it. The initial geotechnical survey therefore included the usual recommendation that the entire foundation structure for the Com-

merzbank should be within the Frankfurt Clay, whose characteristics are well known. It was suggested that the structure should take the form of a raft (to spread the weight over the full area of the site) with piles to control the raft's settlement. Two alternative raft forms were considered: a solid slab 6 metres thick, and a thinner base slab, 2.5 metres thick, stiffened by a grillage of vertical walls three storeys deep. The cellular structure was favoured at this stage as it seemed more likely to fit in with the developing architectural ideas.

The triangular superstructure that was being developed had one particular feature which could only aggravate the difficulty of designing the substructure: the entire weight of the building would be concentrated beneath each of the three towers rather than spread over the whole site. Since it would not be possible to support the towers within the clay layer alone, the only solution was to

devise a transfer structure which would distribute the concentrated loads over the full area of a raft, which could then be piled in the way usual in Frankfurt. Early schemes for the building included three or four levels of basement car parks. These would bring two benefits for the substructure: there would be sufficient depth of basement to effect the redistribution of loads to the raft, and the deep excavation would sufficiently reduce the load on the clay beneath to allow it to carry the weight of the building. On the other hand, the deep basement would leave correspondingly less depth of clay to carry the piles.

It was clear that the overall weight of the building would need to be reduced by every possible means – one designer's question about the weight of door handles was only just a joke. At competition stage, a workable though expensive scheme for the substructure was devised which used a deep, solid raft supported on piles. Nevertheless, it was clear that the new building would need very long piles in a comparatively soft clay and there was concern that the

inevitable settlement of the foundations might threaten adjacent buildings.

As the competition deadline approached, ideas had to converge and the so-called 'fish-tail' option was selected. In this scheme there would be three internal cores at each corner of the triangular plan housing stairs and services risers, while all the lifts would be concentrated in an extension from one corner and ascend on the outside of the building. There had been some talk by the client of future additions to the new building and this separate lift tower would have facilitated this possibility.

In such a tall building it was essential that the floor structure be as thin as possible, and in the office areas between the three towers – the so-called petals – the structural engineers had proposed 16-metre precast-concrete planks spanning between steel beams. The volume occupied by the planks would be used especially efficiently by casting longitudinal voids in the concrete. These would serve as supply and exhaust ducts for the air conditioning. The remaining services would be housed in a deep, raised floor.

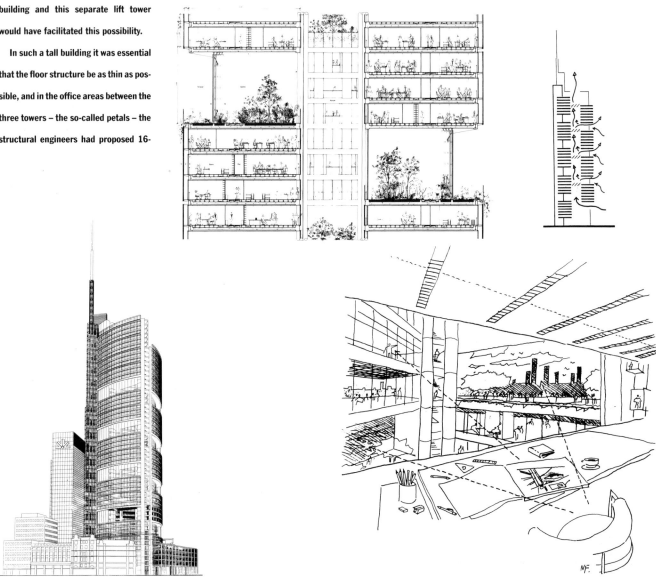

For much of the year the building would be naturally ventilated. To prevent it becoming a 250-metre-tall wind tunnel the full-height atrium was divided into four sections by horizontal glazed screens. Air would flow horizontally through the office floors in the villages, the central void of each nine-storey section, and the gardens. The flow would be limited and adjusted by louvres which would also serve to control smoke in the event of a fire.

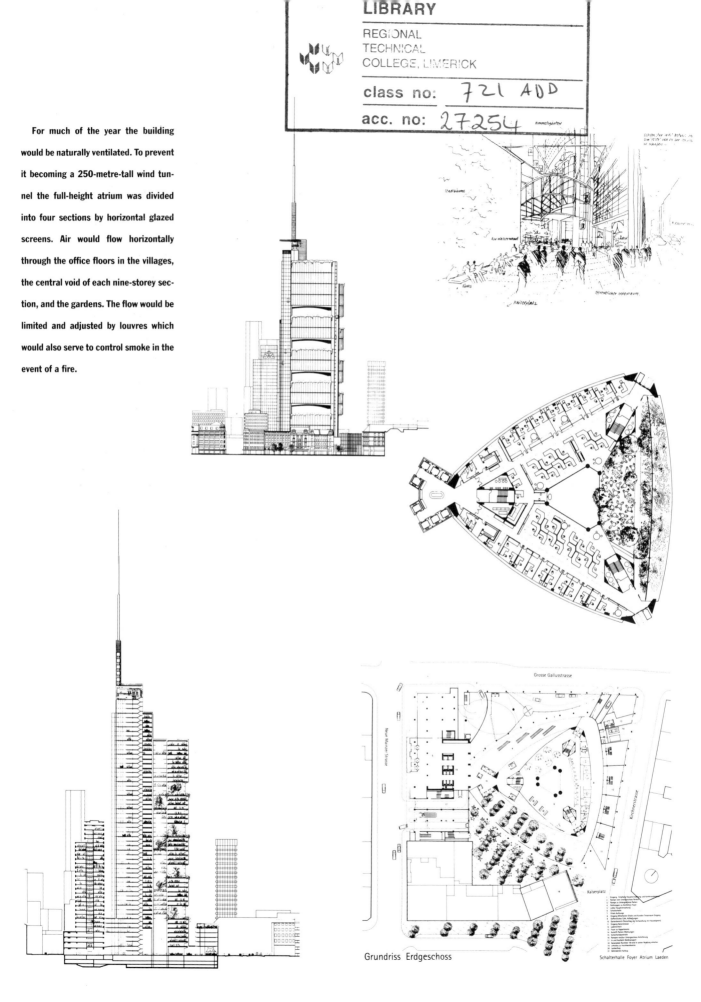

Grundriss Erdgeschoss

Schalterhalle Foyer Atrium Laeden

Design development and integration

The fish-tail scheme was finally selected by the Commerzbank as winner of the Ideas Competition. It was given the go-ahead in late 1991 for further development and final approval in order to secure the necessary building permit.

Further work on the competition scheme exposed some difficulties. The internal structure and services cores were intruding too much on the usable floor space and compromising the ratio of net-to-gross floor areas. Also, the number and location of the lifts were making it difficult to provide suitable vertical transportation. It had been planned to have two sets of lifts: one to serve each six-storey village (arriving at the fourth floor), and others to serve the floors within each village (up two floors and down three).

The response to these problems was to increase the number of lifts in the fish-tail from eight to fourteen, and to reduce the sizes of the cores and move them towards the vertices of the triangular floor plan. But still the scheme was found to have disadvantages. The fish-tail added a large area of building envelope for relatively little enclosed volume. This meant a lot of additional cladding and excessive heat loss in winter, and the location of the lifts and cores meant there were always relatively large distances to walk in any journey between floors.

The shape of the building would also have a serious bearing on the structure. The fins would increase the wind resistance of the building and generate eccentric and torsional loads (both loads would need additional structure to resist them). There were also worries about the proximity of the adjacent building – the fins would be just 5 metres away and such a small gap would lead to very high local wind speeds and negative pressures on adjacent windows. These concerns were not helped by the difficulties below ground level. No matter how carefully the new basements and foundations might be constructed, there was the possibility of disturbing the ground supporting the existing building just a few metres away and affecting its verticality.

And so eventually the fish-tail was abandoned in favour of a three-core solution within a symmetrical plan. Three sets of lifts would serve all floors of the building and the structure and services would be integrated more tightly within the cores to liberate more usable floor space and improve the net-to-gross area ratio. But there were more serious problems ahead.

The client had been collaborating closely and offering encouragement as the original brief evolved to take account of some of the new ideas which had arisen during design development. However, it gradually became clear that the original cost plan was going to be exceeded. Finally, a meeting of the Commerzbank Board decided that the scheme, as it then stood, was too expensive and did not make efficient enough use of the gross floor area.

In response to this decision, and before focusing their efforts to improve the scheme, the building designers undertook a detailed comparison of eight possible versions of the building with different building plans, floor layouts, structural and core details, and servicing and lifting strategies. These were compared with respect to cost, programme time, foundations, ease of construction, net-to-gross efficiency, and environmental issues.

Following this comparative study, the architects set up independent design teams to develop two of the alternative strategies. One team would work on the current scheme with the modified brief and strive to bring it back within budget and make the floor use more efficient. The other team would develop an idea which had been previously discarded – a more conventional scheme with a single, central core with the garden areas at the corners of the triangular plan. The result was a double success. A central-core scheme was developed at considerably less than the original budget and with a better net-to-gross area ratio; and the three-core scheme was also brought back on budget with a better net-to-gross ratio and improved transport strategy. While the central-core scheme was rather cheaper it offered a less attractive solution from the point of view of workplace and environmental issues. The client was by this time sufficiently wedded to the more innovative three-core scheme to favour it, as long as it could be delivered on budget.

The various improvements to the three-core competition scheme were achieved mainly by a change to the building footprint and a number of developments to the building services. The efficiency of floor use was improved by changing the rounded triangular footprint to one with rather flatter faces. The servicing in the competition scheme had used on-floor plant. Although this offered great flexibility, it was hungry on floor space. By centralising the building services into two main plant rooms the core areas of the building could be better exploited and the net-to-gross area ratio improved. The number of storeys in each village was increased from six to eight, and the height of the gardens from three to four storeys. This gained some floor area and enabled the lifting strategy to be improved. The number of full-height lifts was reduced to just two, for the disabled and goods. The other lifts would serve selected floors – one group for floors 1–21, a second for 22–35, and a third for 35–50. The space above and between these short-run lifts was liberated to gain yet more usable floor area.

The reduced number of villages and gardens brought a number of other benefits. More daylight would be brought into the interior of the building and less equipment would be needed to control airflow through the gardens and central void. The new scheme also resulted in a less abrupt top to the building, which the city planners favoured in such a prominent structure.

In general, the existing structural scheme was adaptable enough to accommodate all these various changes with only minor alterations, and the larger size of the villages did permit

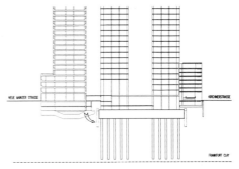

Competition scheme – solid, piled raft

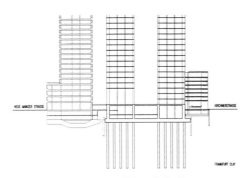

Revised scheme – cellular, piled raft

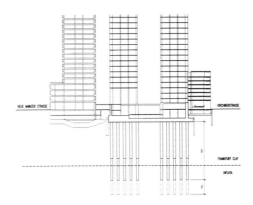

Final scheme – fully piled, no raft

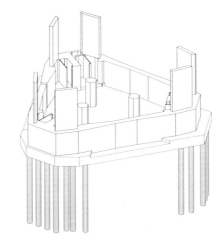

Final scheme

some small reductions in the size, and hence, cost, of the frame structure. However, one of the ways in which the cost of the building was brought back on budget was to have very serious consequences for the design of the foundations.

It had been decided to move the basement car-parking to one of the perimeter buildings in order to reduce the number of basement levels to two beneath the tower and one elsewhere. The foundations of the competition scheme were at the very limit of what could be achieved using a piled raft. Reducing the number of basements would mean that less soil would need to be excavated and the ground beneath would have to carry additional weight; since this would give rise to excessive settlements a piled raft would no longer be feasible. An entirely new foundation structure would have to be devised, one which would be unprecedented in the Frankfurt area.

The first approach was to try to refine the substructure incorporated within the bottom three storeys of the tower, one above and two below ground level. As in the competition scheme, the cellular transfer structure, comprising a grid of 12-metre-deep shear walls, would distribute the loads from the main columns over the full area of soil beneath the tower. However, it was found to be very difficult to make good use of these lower storeys unless a large number of openings were provided through the shear walls; this reduced their structural effectiveness so much that, once again, the foundations could not be made to work at an acceptable cost.

And so the bullet had to be bitten – an answer would have to found at greater depth; piles would have to penetrate the Inflata layer and a whole new world would need to be explored. Once this decision had been made, some tremendous benefits followed. It was quickly recognised that there was no longer any need for the usual raft. The load paths through the foundation could be made significantly simpler and cheaper – loads from the three cores could be carried vertically right down to the piles rather than having to be diverted through 90° into the raft and a further 90° into the piles. Also, since the internal stiffening walls of the cellular raft would now be redundant, they could be removed and free up the interior space in the basements.

Full three-storey-deep stiffening walls were retained in the circumference to give fixity to the feet of the main columns of the tower. And, since the perimeter buildings now had only one basement, the walls of the lower basement beneath the tower would not need to be penetrated by circulation and service routes. This solid 4-metre-deep wall would be able to provide sufficient stiffness to allow the rest of the stiffening walls to be penetrated more freely. the provision of an entire storey of unpenetrated wall had not been possible in the earlier, cellular raft schemes and, with hindsight, this was found to bring much greater flexibility to the planning of services and circulation routes between the

tower and the perimeter buildings on the two storeys above.

As the piles for this foundation scheme would be longer (between 40 and 50 metres) than could be achieved using conventional piling equipment, a new type of pile had to be devised. The main problem would be to overcome friction in the 30 metres of clay when piling at greater depth. The solution was to adopt a step reduction in the pile diameter just above the Inflata layer. An oversize hole was cut through the clay and lined; this allowed the smaller hole to be cut into the Inflata layer without being impeded by friction in the clay above.

With these more fundamental issues dealt with, the process of refining the scheme in all its details and reducing its cost could begin. A computer spreadsheet program was written to perform a large number of 'what-if' tests on the Vierendeel structure of each village to find the best compromise between the ideal forms for gravity loads and wind loads. In this way the maximum feasible stiffness per tonne was extracted from the steel. At the same time the location of the connections between the steel members was considered; by positioning them at or near points of contraflexure (where bending moments are zero) they would need to carry mainly shear loads and could be correspondingly lighter, simpler, cheaper and easier to assemble in situ.

The floor system in the petal areas also needed to be reconsidered. The structural engineers came to realise that stitching each of the concrete floor

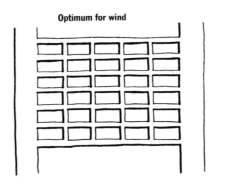

Optimum for wind

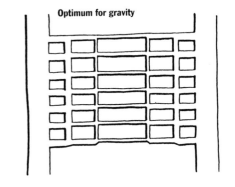

Optimum for gravity

Bending moments and splice locations

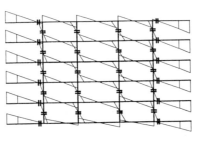

Wind loading

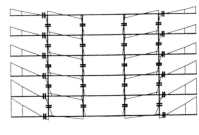

Gravity loading

planks containing air ducts to the main structural frame would require considerable time and effort, which would be correspondingly costly. It was also found that this did not bring the weight advantage which had been anticipated. The engineers proposed an all-steel alternative (a metal decking floor on steel beams) which would be lighter, easier to construct and cheaper. However, even this change was not straightforward. The beams would need to be perforated by a large number of holes to accommodate the air ducts – five or six in a 16-metre length – and this would be too costly. Attention was again focused on the services. The entire system of ventilation and air conditioning was reassessed to design out some of them services and so reduce the number of ducts beneath floors and bring costs back within budget.

This amount of steel in the building brought two problems. The first was cultural: it is still the norm in Germany to make large buildings from concrete and most German contractors were not keen to construct in steel. The second concerned the dynamic behaviour of the building in gusty wind conditions. The building would need to be made stiff enough to ensure the frequency of oscillation, and the accelerations would need to be low enough to be acceptable to occupants. Being an all-steel building, and hence very light, it would be more sensitive to wind loads than a heavier building (the acceleration due to a force varies inversely with the mass). But as this problem is solved by increasing the

stiffness, so the frequency of oscillation increases. There was also the question of damping. Since steel is highly elastic, oscillations of the building caused by wind gusts die down very slowly.

A detailed study was undertaken to

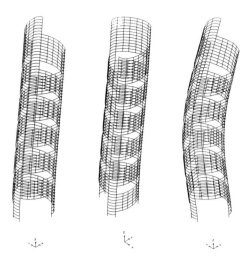

investigate the dynamic behaviour of the structure, both in the direction of the wind and perpendicular to it. The stiffness was adjusted to limit the maximum acceleration in a ten-year period to 1.5 per cent of the acceleration due to gravity – rather less than the recommended levels. Sufficient damping was introduced into the building by making the main load-bearing columns in the cores from reinforced concrete, which absorbs much more energy than steel when it vibrates. The concrete would also encase the steel corner columns of the Vierendeel frames, and shear studs welded to the columns would ensure composite action with the concrete.

The client still had reservations about the all-steel structural scheme, partly because of the preference for concrete in Germany. To satisfy these concerns, an all-concrete alternative was prepared

on lines similar to the current steel design. It was found that the vertical elements of the Vierendeels would need to be nearly 2 metres wide and nearly half the window area would be lost. The building would also be some 20 per cent heavier and no cost-effective foundation could be devised which would carry this weight. A concrete version of the building would simply not be feasible.

The construction method devised by the structural engineers will have minimum impact on the environment and be as cost-effective as possible. Below ground, matters will be dominated by the nature of the soil and the Inflata layer beneath, the proximity of the adjacent building and the high water table, which must not be disturbed. Concrete piles cast inside temporary casings will be used in preference to the less environmentally-friendly Bentonite. Vertical and horizontal movement of the soft clay soil will be minimised by undertaking a ballasted excavation of the site – as soil is removed, the surface will be surcharged with new construction to maintain soil pressures and prevent heave. By this means the foundations of the adjacent high-rise building and several listed buildings will be protected.

Above ground the entire design of the structure has been conceived with rapid and cheap construction in mind. Only the nine triangular steel columns and the small frames linking each pair of concrete columns change in size down the building. The rest of the structure is virtually identical at every floor level throughout the 250-metre height. Even the six main reinforced-concrete columns are of constant external dimensions – their increasing strength and stiffness is achieved by adjusting the internal reinforcement.

This repetition is made possible because the building is braced by Vierendeel action – it resists wind loads by shearing rather than bending. Hence the resistance to wind is shared more or less equally by the structure at each floor level rather than progressively accumulating in the columns towards ground level (as is the case in a building which resists wind by bending). The floor and Vierendeel structure of each village is designed, first and foremost, as a kit of parts to facilitate easy construction. Steelwork will be cut, drilled, welded and prefabricated in factory conditions, with as few different components and sub-assemblies as possible. All connections are made with friction grip bolts to avoid site welding. It has thus been possible to

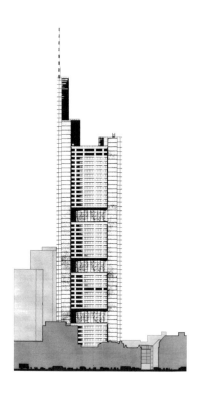

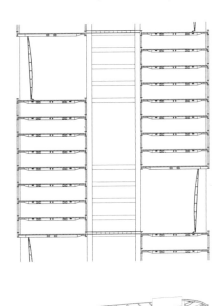

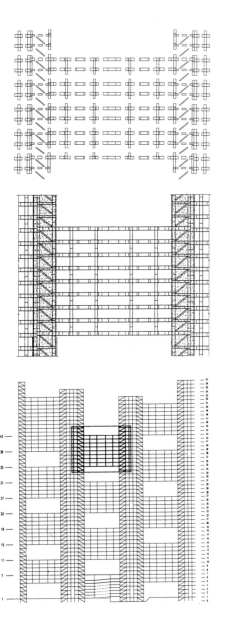

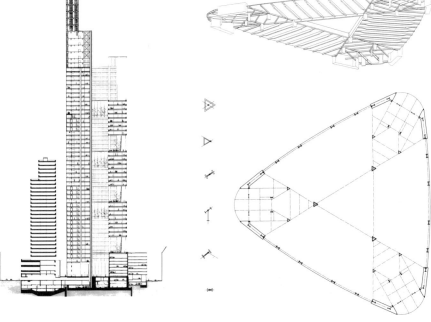

achieve an unprecedented degree of standardisation in such a tall building.

Design of the new Commerzbank headquarters was substantially complete by the end of 1993, some 24 months after the competition had been won and the building completed towards the end of 1996. The building which has resulted from the imaginative brief is a highly-engineered building which, to quote one of its designers, 'breaks all the rules'. For a building of its height and type, many of its features are highly original:

- the weight of the entire building (52–61 storeys, about 100,000 tonnes) is just two-thirds that of an adjacent 30-storey block (about 150,000 tonnes);
- it carries gravity and wind loads in original ways;
- its fully piled foundation is unique and of unprecedented depth in Frankfurt;
- the structure has a highly-repetitive kit of parts and sub-assemblies with standardised dimensions and connections;
- it is the first major steel building in Germany;
- it is the first major high-rise building in Germany with dry walling;
- the floor utilisation is very high – each floor accommodates 60 office units at 15 m^2 per person;
- the office space is entirely column-free;
- its shape in plan provides very large window areas for the site and floor area;
- all the offices are naturally lit;
- the building affords striking views from both the inside and ground level;
- while being a large building it does not appear as a monolithic block and has

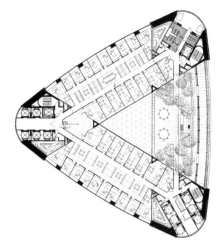

an entrance which is in harmony with the scale of the surrounding buildings;

- for about nine months of the year it is naturally ventilated;
- the gardens give fresh air quality right to the top of the building.

Further reading

The Structural Engineer, 2 April 1996

Ponds Forge
International Sports Centre

Sheffield 1991

Structural engineer for roof   John Gregory, Neil Carstairs

Ove Arup & Partners

Architect   FaulknerBrowns

Client   Sheffield City Council

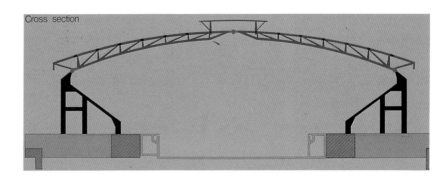

Cross section

The idea for the roof over the pool at Ponds Forge had its origins in the ribs of a Gothic, vaulted masonry roof. In the modern context, the ribs are curved steel girders forming a three-pin arch, though this is not an arch in the structural sense since the girders must withstand substantial bending as well as pure compression. The girders (which, on structural grounds, could have been straight) are pinned at each end of the span and where they meet in the centre. By making the joints in the form of hinges, turning moments in one axis are virtually eliminated. A further advantage of the three-pin arch is that changes of temperature, rather than leading to large stresses within the structure and the need for heavier members, can be accommodated by the movement of the roof. Pin-joints are one of many means by which a structural engineer can make a structure behave in a prescribed and, hence, better understood way; they also make the structural analysis easier.

The roof spans nearly 55 metres and is extremely flat. This was achieved largely by incorporating all the ventilation equipment and ducts beneath and behind the seating rather than hanging from the roof – the headroom could thus be lower and the structure lighter since it needs to carry a smaller imposed load. However, the large span-to-rise ratio (8.7) leads to very large lateral thrusts on the side supports.

The eaves joint had to be designed to transmit a total of some 330 tonnes from the two roof trusses, which meet at 55° on plan, to the concrete abutment. It was necessary to incorporate a pin-joint in one axis and a spherical bearing to permit lateral twisting when the roof is loaded asymmetrically. The joint also had to carry the tubular struts which support the upper member of the trusses where they project outwards beyond the hinge.

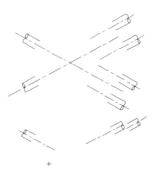 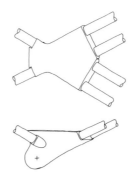 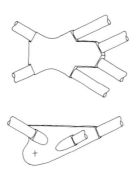 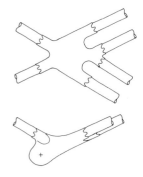

A casting was preferred from the outset for this important joint as it would allow the freedom to sculpt a functional and visually striking component. The design evolved through many versions, from the raw geometric requirements to an arrangement which was well-suited to the casting process, provided the most streamlined load path through the casting, avoided awkward welds between tubes and the casting, and which would use as little metal as possible. The result was a connection that was cheaper than the fabricated alternative.

Although the casting is solid, apart from the obvious holes, it is designed to carry the loads in its outer shell so that the small flaws inevitable in castings could be more easily detected and repaired. Loads from the tubes are transferred to the casting through a circumferential weld, whose detail is perhaps not immediately apparent.

After fabrication the outer end of each roof truss was left with three bare tubes, the bottom pair of which would be received by the eaves casting when lowered in situ. As it would clearly be difficult to manoeuvre the heavy and unwieldy truss and slot the tubes into circular sockets, the casting was made with the top half of each socket absent. It was thus possible to locate the truss tubes precisely by simply lowering them into the waiting socket cups and welding the tubes and the top half of the cups in position. However, if the sockets had had straight ends, the weld joining the casting to the tube would not have been long enough to carry the forces from tube to

casting. By forming a scalloped end, the length of the weld was increased by about 50 per cent.

At the other end of the casting, unsightly holding-down bolts were avoided by designing the connection as a compression joint and cementing the hollow shell of the casting onto the concrete frame, rather in the manner of a crown glued onto the stub of a tooth.

Further reading

The Architects' Journal, 17 July 1991
pp. 43–45
Arup Journal, Vol. 26 No. 2, 1991,
pp. 3–9

Don Valley Stadium

Sheffield 1990

Structural engineer	Anthony Hunt, Steve Morley
	<u>YRM-Anthony Hunt Associates</u>
	<u>(Sheffield)</u>
Architect	<u>Design and Building Services,</u>
	Sheffield City Council
Client	<u>Sheffield for Health</u>

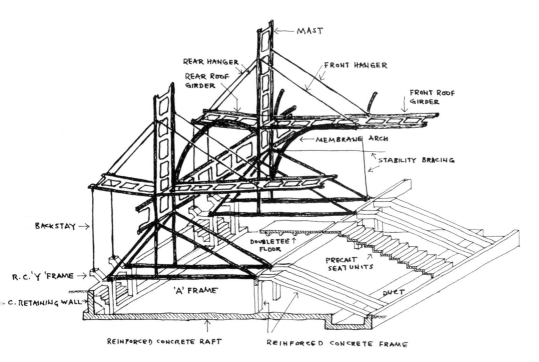

Labels: MAST · REAR HANGER · FRONT HANGER · REAR ROOF GIRDER · FRONT ROOF GIRDER · MEMBRANE ARCH · STABILITY BRACING · BACKSTAY · DOUBLE TEE FLOOR · PRECAST SEAT UNITS · R.C. 'Y' FRAME · C. RETAINING WALL · 'A' FRAME · DUCT · REINFORCED CONCRETE RAFT · REINFORCED CONCRETE FRAME

alternative shapes were considered by architect and engineer and the final choice was a series of saddles between the masts with a conical form at the corners.

With such high stress involved it is imperative that the membrane is cut and sewn in precisely the right shape so that over-stressing and slack areas are avoided entirely. The shape of this type of membrane can be controlled by adjusting the levels of the radial and hoop stresses and the geometry of the boundaries; in particular, the stresses and shape are very sensitive to the diameter of the central hole. First of all, a computer program finds the form that a

A roof over a grandstand gives both architect and engineer the rare opportunity to expose the heart and soul of a building's structure. As an acknowledgement to the heritage of the city and the site (a former steelworks), steel is used in the form of simple cantilevers to support a translucent structural-membrane roof over the 10,000-seat main grandstand. As perceived by the public the roof is a 'simple' tent structure supported by a steel frame. The section of the roof cantilevered over the spectators is kept in balance by the steel cable tying the steel frame down to the back of the stand. At this level the entire structural concept is plain to see.

At a deeper level, the story is more complex – the stresses in the roof membrane are hundreds of times higher than in an ordinary tent and a substantial supporting frame was needed. Also, because wind loads on such a roof are large and varied, some elements of the

supporting structure, which look as though they will only ever carry tensile forces, need on occasions to carry large compression forces.

As the client required the membrane to have a long life in service, a relatively new material was chosen. Teflon-coated woven glass fibre is both durable and strong; it weighs just 1.6 kg/m^2 and has an ultimate tensile strength of 16 tonnes per metre width. Although 93 per cent opaque, the fabric is noticeably translucent both by day and by night; grey in its early life, it is slowly bleached by sunlight and, being 'non-stick', tends not to attract dirt.

A membrane structure needs be tensioned throughout its surface in order to prevent fluttering in wind or large deflections under wind and snow loads. This is achieved by using a doubly-curved (anticlastic) shape which, unlike its ancestor, the tent, can be highly prestressed (to 0.5 tonnes per metre). A number of

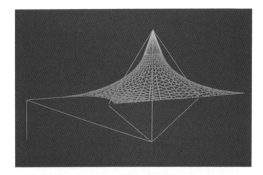

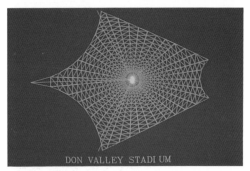

DON VALLEY STADIUM

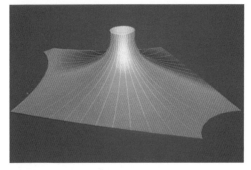

membrane would take up with uniform tension in all directions. This process is the mathematical equivalent of lifting the centre of a flat soap bubble using a circular loop – if the central loop is too small, or lifted too much, the bubble bursts (in computing terms, the iterative calculation does not converge on an equilibrium state). The results can nowadays be represented on a computer screen and a shape which is neither too flat nor with pronounced necking can be selected visually. Having found a suitable shape, the computer model of the form is combined with a model of the material properties of the elastic membrane to generate a new, slightly different equilibrium shape. The distribution of stresses in the membrane is calculated and can also be displayed visually; if these are too high or too low the process can be repeated with new input data. Lastly, a series of patterns is computed to enable panels of the membrane material to be cut and sewn to create the correct final form.

The membrane in the corner cones is prestressed by a three-dimensional system of cables and struts. These, too, needed to be designed using a mathematical model to balance the stresses in the membrane with those in the pre-stressing structure.

It was noted that the required training facilities, which included an indoor running track, could be located under the main grandstand and so save both building area and cost: but how, then, would the roof mast, seating and concourse be supported. The solution was to reflect, at the rear, the raking beams which support the seating at the front and link them by a horizontal tie at concourse level to form a structurally-efficient tied A-frame. This same clear expression of forces was used in the simple front hanger and backstay arrangement which supports the 26-metre roof cantilevers.

Further reading

Structural Engineering International, Vol. 2, April 1992

Inland Revenue Offices

Nottingham 1993

Structural engineer   John Thornton, **Ove Arup & Partners**

Architect: **Michael Hopkins & Partners**

Client: **Inland Revenue**

Elegance and simplicity seldom come about by chance; they must generally be set early on as a specific goal, and much experience, effort and skill must be directed towards achieving that goal. With hindsight it is easy to suppose that a simple solution to a design problem was obvious – 'I could have thought of that.'

To do this is often to render invisible the very process of design and, unfortunately, is a habit common among non-designers.

What could be simpler, then, than the superstructure of the Inland Revenue offices?

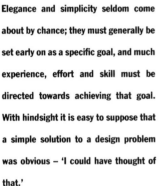

1 Prepare the site and foundations ready for columns.

2 Construct the building cores of in-situ concrete.

3 Deliver and erect fully-finished brick-work columns, working away from the cores.

4 Deliver and erect fully-finished pre-cast-concrete floor slabs.

5 Repeat steps 3 and 4 for second and third floors.

Perhaps not quite that simple, but certainly an important step forward in showing how building construction can benefit from the lessons of production

engineering learnt in other industries. With intelligence and forethought it is <u>not</u> inevitable that off-site manufacture and prefabrication produce identical components and monotonous buildings.

The production process for the brick-work columns was conceived to enable a range of similar but different units to be created.

The steel and timber formwork for the precast-concrete vaults was made in sections. A series of inserts allowed for variations such as the end details or holes for light fittings. In this manner nearly 900 units, in two basic sizes with a total of 120 variants, could be manu-

factured economically and with a high-quality surface finish.

The vaulted ceiling has its ancestry in the brick jack-arches spanning between the cast- or wrought-iron beams that were so ubiquitous in 19th-century warehouses and mills. But the similarity between the two systems is little more than geometric. In the mills the vault is an arch both in form and structural action, and the iron beams seldom span more than 3 or 4 metres between iron columns and masonry walls; the walls provide the lateral stability. The modern concrete 'vault' is actually a folded-plate slab that spans some 13 metres between

masonry columns; lateral stability is provided by the in-situ-concrete cores.

The shape of the concrete vaults had another derivation. Modern fire regulations limit the minimum thickness of a concrete slab to 95 mm; taking into account the ease of getting the steel and concrete into the formwork, the minimum practical thickness is about 130 mm. But a slab that thin could span no more than about 3 metres. How, then, could this minimum thickness of concrete be used to form a lightweight beam that was stiff and strong enough to span the full 13 metres? The solution was to increase the stiffness of the section (second moment of area) by corrugating the slab. What could be simpler?

Further reading

<u>The Architects' Journal</u>, 16 June 1993, pp. 41–52

D.G. Bank, Pariserplatz

Berlin 1999

Structural engineer   Schlaich Bergermann and Partners

Architect   Frank O. Gehry

Client   D. G. Bank

As young engineers we learn that the best shape for an arch or a dome is found by creating a hanging structure, and then inverting it; this avoids bending and creates a pure compression structure. However, this is only the case for the gravity loads; real structures have to carry wind loads too which means that all such structures need to have some bending stiffness. In fact, this introduces more freedom in design since the architect is not forced to choose the catenary or parabolic shapes of funicular structures. If the form deviates only a little from the funicular shape, adequate stiffness can be provided in the joints of the lattice. For a larger deviation from the funicular, or large wind loads, the shape can be stiffened using ties. The principal constraint for glazed roofs of moderate span becomes a geometric one: how can a curved surface be created using flat facets of glass, recalling the obvious fact that any three points are in a plane, while four points need not be.

This free-form sculptural roof by Frank Gehry could only be created using triangular panes on a triangular grid throughout. This also allowed the vault still to appear curved where the curvature is very tight. Most of the roof's stiffness is provided by the stainless steel nodes, which are milled from solid to generate the many different angles between lattice members. In the longitudinal direction

the curvature is slight and so little stiffness is provided by shell action in this direction. The necessary additional stiffness is provided by two sets of radial ties. The vault is supported at only four places along its length – at the ends and at two intermediate arches which contain the rings of radial ties. This allows the structure to appear to float free of the building and, indeed, sink below the horizontal at one end.

Further reading
Journal of IASS, Vol. 40, No. 3, 1999

Hippopotamus house, Berlin Zoo

Structural engineer   Schlaich Bergermann and Partners

Architect   Jörg Gribl

Client   Zoological Garden, Berlin

Berlin 1997

The new glass enclosure for the hippopotamus house at Berlin Zoo needed two areas about 29 and 21 metres in diameter for hippos and dwarf hippos. There are many ways to span over a circular plan. The most popular in the nineteenth century was to use radial ribs, but this has the disadvantage that many ribs congregate at the centre, which is where the visitor would like greatest transparency. It is also difficult to link two such forms, which was a particular wish of the architect. It was also preferred to use quadrangular glass panes to create greater overall transparency.

The design engineers devised their solution using a surface generated by moving a single generator curve along another curve, the directrix. These are called translational surfaces and have

the great advantage that they generate flat quadrangular panes. The circular plan was developed by choosing a parabola as the generatrix and the same parabola (at right-angles) as the directrix. The surface lining the large and small domes could be generated using a transition curve to link the two parabolas of different sizes. On the south face of the building the doubly-curved roof intersects with an inverted cone to form the transparent wall.

A further advantage of these structural forms, of which the hyperbolic paraboloid is the best known particular example, is that they carry their loads in the plane of the surface, across the diagonals of the quadrangles. These loads are carried by a net of diagonal steel cables, which impair the transparency of

the structure very little. This method of generating structural forms gives the engineer and architect enormous flexibility and far greater freedom of choice than using funicular shapes or forms generated by simple rotation, such as spheres and ellipsoids.

Further reading
Stahlbau, Vol. 67, 1998
Structural Engineering International, April 1997

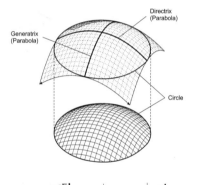

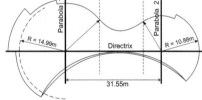

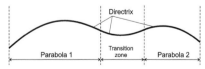

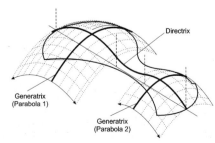

Wind impinging on the communication dishes and exposed faces of the equipment floors can impose considerable torsion loads on the tower. The outriggers, which also support the equipment floors, are designed as cantilevers on plan to transmit the torsion loads from the perimeter of the tower to the central, reinforced-concrete core. The tubular cross-section of the core – a constant internal diameter of 3 metres and wall thickness varying from 750 mm at the base to just 300 mm at the top of the truss – is the most efficient type of structure to conduct the torsion loads down to the foundations.

In the vertical plane of the basic truss are three sets of diagonals. These serve two purposes: they stiffen the upper portion of the tower, which effectively acts as a cantilever above the level of the guys; and they carry the weight of the twelve equipment floors and their imposed loads back to the central concrete core. This substantially reduces the forces that the trussing wires have to carry.

The guys that stabilise the tower, being cables, are unable to withstand compression forces, and yet the possibility of the guys going slack when the tower is subject to high wind loads had

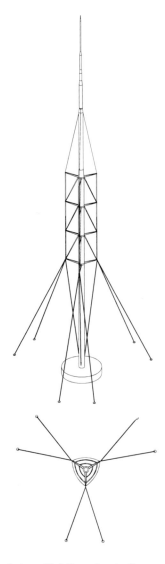

built on flat land, a further subtlety to the design of the guys was needed. Had they all been of the same cross-section, the shorter guys would have been stiffer and thus attracted a disproportionately large share of the total load being carried. The shorter guys were made less stiff to match the elasticity of the longer ones by reducing the number of strands in the steel cable.

Wind loads on such a tall, exposed tower are high – up to 5 kN/m^2 at the top – and the equipment floors present to the wind about the same area as a 25-storey office block. Wind tunnel tests were done on the tower to investigate both the wind flows over the landscape and the air flow around the equipment floors themselves. These helped to jus-

tify the theoretical assumptions about wind loading and to ensure that small wind eddies would not set the tower or its elements into dangerous oscillation (which caused the collapse of the Tacoma Narrows suspension bridge in 1940). These tests enabled the weight of the tower, and of the equipment floors in particular, to be substantially reduced. It weighs about 2700 tonnes, a third of the weight of an equivalent 7500 square-metre terrestrial office block. The light weight also eased the task of raising the 12-storey block from ground level, where it was built, into its final position 85 metres up the tower.

Further reading

The Structural Engineer, 19 October 1993, pp. 353–358
The Architects' Journal, 17 June 1992, pp. 22–23

to be avoided. By prestressing the guys against the central concrete tube, which is a structural form well able to carry compressive loads, a guy can, effectively, be made to carry a compressive force by having its pretension force reduced.

Rather than the absolute minimum of three guys, six (three splayed pairs) are used. These give a margin of safety as protection against the horrific consequences should one of only three cables be severely damaged; they also provide some additional torsional stiffness to the structure in plan. Since the tower is not

Without prestressing

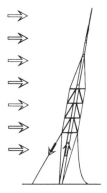

With prestressing

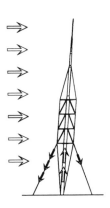

Buildings need to be, above all, functional. Engineers have tended in the past to take this rather literally and narrowly – beams that carry their loads without causing plastered ceilings to crack, piles that carry loads from the building into the soil, roofs that safely carry snow loads and wind uplift. However, this type of function is probably not what the owner or user of the building has in mind – to them function means how the building serves their needs. This might be having a large span between columns, or a roof with more headroom in the centre than at the eaves, or having large areas of north light fenestration, or a structural form that facilitates natural ventilation. It might be having a building that can be easily adaptable to a new use. These functions are also important for the architect, whose task is to collaborate with the engineer to provide these functions for the client. However, the architect will probably have an additional agenda – the creation of a building of architectural merit in its own right, which may in turn, of course, serve the owner well when it attracts critical acclaim.

Focusing on the client's needs broadens the picture for the engineer. No longer is it enough to try to create a structure that is good in its own terms. It must also be judged according to the client's value system – how it helps the client get the function or performance he needs, or to get it more quickly, or at lower cost. This change of perception during the last decade or two has dramatically altered the context in which structural engineers work. In particular it has heightened the need for engineers – both structures and services – to be involved right at the beginning of the design process to ensure that their contribution can be most influential and effective.

Building users seldom want the structure of a building, any more than they want radiators or chillers. They want a comfortable and safe environment – well lit, a suitable temperature but not stuffy, dry and quiet, with suitable interior spaces and access, local control of light and ventilation, and so on. Together this list amounts to a performance specification, but not one that is directed only to the structural engineer, or the services engineer or architect either. The fact of the matter is that the performance the occupier wants can only be delivered when the various engineering systems are working together and in harmony.

The building owner or developer has a slightly different perception again. Unlike the occupier, they are also interested in the construction phase, the maintenance and adaptability of the building in the longer term. This all adds to the need for integrated planning and design for the whole life of a building.

The concrete shell is among the most remarkable achievements in structural engineering history – alongside the masonry arch, the flying buttress and the I-beam. However, the circumstances when it can nowadays be the best choice are limited – it is opaque, must conform precisely to a geometry imposed by statics and is labour-intensive to construct. When all this suits the building use, it is both elegant and efficient. Heinz Isler has exploited a niche market for his shells among building owners who have these requirements – petrol stations, DIY stores, garden centres and indoor sports, as illustrated in this chapter. The aviary in Hong Kong, the exhibition hall at Hannover and the new acoustic wall at Gatwick Airport in London all exploit structural forms that suit their function. The arch-supported cable net easily follows the irregular ground profile and provides a structure with minimal visual impact on this inner-city site in Hong Kong. At Hannover, the long span of the catenary and its striking image influenced the client's choice for the new exhibition hall at the massive trade exhibition park. It needed to be functional, distinctive and economical. At Gatwick a wave-form structure provides acoustic screening and blast protection using pre-cast concrete which was erected quickly and economically with minimum disturbance to the busy airport.

Air-inflated ETFE-foil cushions offer a roofing system with excellent inherent building environmental characteristics. These cushions are extremely lightweight, transparent or translucent, excellent thermal insulators and transparent to sound, which can prevent the unpleasant acoustic associated with swimming pools and some other indoor sports. The atrium roof at Westminster and Chelsea Hospital illustrates one system for supporting these cushions. They have recently been used at the Eden Centre in Cornwall to create the largest enclosed botanic garden in the world (Engineers: Anthony Hunt Associates and Buro Happold; Architect: Nicholas Grimshaw and Partners).

The new headquarters building for James Dyson's vacuum cleaner factory illustrates how a simple 'shed' can be transformed into a unique, economical and characterful building which will allow the owner considerable flexibility as the firm develops and changes. The new laboratory complex for Schlumberger at Cambridge is a prestige building drawing heavily for its impact on the distinctive architecture. Reflecting the engineering business of its owner, the exposed structure displays the engineering aesthetic of the materials while providing an attractive, functional and highly-serviced research environment. The Presbyterian church in New York and the Royal Court Theatre in London, on the other hand, are examples of old buildings of character given new and extended lives through the ingenuity of engineers who found ways to adapt them to new uses.

Imaginative engineering is given its greatest stimulus, perhaps, when the building function is unique and there is little precedent to draw upon. The Haj airport terminal at Jeddah is truly enormous, providing temporary shade for up to 80,000 pilgrims. The ventilation problem is equally enormous and the use of the natural form of the membrane canopies to help create the necessary updraft was an inspired interaction of the structural and ventilation systems. At the research base in the Antarctic the need to transport a building in kit form was paramount and it was intelligently decided to separate the structural and insulation functions by housing the habitable quarters inside a flexible timber tube. The final example in this chapter, a child's tree-house, is structural engineering at its simplest, but the thinking behind the structural system – the elegant avoidance of large loads rather than providing a large and cumbersome structure – is as ingenious as found in many a larger building.

Norwich Sport Village

1987

Structural engineer   <u>Heinz Isler</u>

Architect   <u>Copeland Associates</u>
in conjunction with
<u>Haus & Herd</u>

During the last quarter of a century, perhaps for the first time in about two thousand years, virtually no compression roof structures have been built. Roman domes and barrel vaults, Gothic vaults and baroque domes (and their copies) were ubiquitous until well into this century. From the 1940s, reinforced concrete in the form of a variety of thin shells was able to continue the tradition, using both a new material and developments in engineering science which enabled the behaviour and stability of such shells to be confirmed and justified. The bold displays by Maillart, Candela, Nervi and Torroja (engineers all) of what could be achieved with concrete shells might well have been the inspiration in the late 1950s for Utzøn (an architect) to propose his Sydney Opera House. Unfortunately, the shape of the roof he imagined was not suitable to work as a structural thin shell: the roof would need to develop significant bend-

ing moments to withstand gravity and wind loads. It required an unprecedented onslaught by highly skilled and mathematically-talented engineers from Ove Arup & Partners, using the recently developed electronic computer, to make the scheme work at all – by disguising a stiff folded-plate structure beneath a smooth exterior. Nevertheless, this project progressed the understanding of shell behaviour substantially and for a decade or so many more such structures were built. Since the 1970s, however, they have largely fallen out of favour; the labour- and material-intensive process of casting in-situ concrete is usually said to be to blame. The need for above-average mathematical skills might have contributed too.

Meanwhile, in Switzerland, Heinz Isler continued to develop and build concrete shells as if he had not heard they were no longer in fashion. He took a highly experimental approach, drawing upon physical analogues to create his forms, in particular Hooke's observation that a hanging chain or net would, if inverted, form a stable compression arch, vault or

dome. Gaudí had used such models in the 1890s to develop the form of the vaults for his cathedral of the Sagrada Familia in Barcelona. More recently Frei Otto and others at the Institute for Lightweight Structures in Stuttgart have experimented with hanging nets in their search for structures which find their own form, and used these to devise appropriate shapes for compression timber grid-shells.

Isler came upon the shapes made by hanging fabrics rather by chance. Although he found them attractive, in themselves, he also realised that, when inverted, they could offer a means of

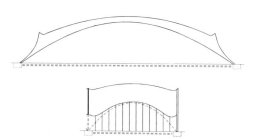

Client   IHS Sport Villages plc/
          Broadland District Council
          Joint Venture

mesh – and the insulation is then attached to this using a plastic fixing (to reduce cold bridging) and stainless-steel wire. Much more reinforcement is needed in the vicinity of the supports.

The concrete mix contains both plasticiser and retarder, allowing it to be worked by hand during the two days needed to pour and finish each shell. After a further few days the roof is given an initial prestress in the perimeter ground beams which pull the corners a little towards each other. After 21 days when the concrete has developed sufficient strength, the remaining prestress is applied by pulling the corners in a little further; this causes the entire shell to be lifted off its centering. This prestress also ensures that the shell does not deflect under its own weight or snow load in a way that would bring part of the concrete surface into tension: good water resistance with no further treatment is thus ensured.

creating the form of a compression shell. He did some simple experiments using lacquer and, later, ice to stiffen garden netting hung from a few supports. After finding the resulting shells remarkably stiff for their thickness, he developed the modelling process to form the basis of a viable design procedure

for full-size structures. Using such physical models has the enormous advantage that it is not necessary to penetrate deeply into mathematics to find families of possible shapes for shells. Indeed, unlike cylindrical and hyperbolic-paraboloid shells, these hanging shapes cannot be described geometrically using a few mathematical equations, which means that an engineer could not analyse them anyway.

By establishing the form using a model, the statical design has only to ensure that the shell is thick enough to withstand local buckling and the stress concentrations which arise at the edges

of the shell and around the supports at ground level. Using models about 500 mm wide, Isler applies a uniform load to an elastic sheet and measures the deformed shape to an accuracy of about one twentieth of a millimetre. The dimensions are then scaled up fifty or a hundred times to the size of the shell to be constructed and used as the basis for setting out the formwork for the concrete. Each shell of the sports hall at Norwich spans some 48 metres to cover a usable floor area of 37 x 18.5 metres.

One of the keys to Isler's success with shells – he has constructed many hundreds since 1955 – is the standardised formwork elements he has helped to develop. These can be used repeatedly on one project, or adapted for reuse on new projects. Glulam timber beams are supported on steel trestles and thin strips of timber layed across the beams. On this layer is placed what will become the interior surface of the roof – slabs of wood-wool and sometimes sprayed polyurethane insulation. Upon this is placed the steel reinforcement – generally two layers of 6 mm steel in a 100 mm

Further reading

Concrete Quarterly, No. 173, summer 1992, pp. 24–26
Concrete Quarterly, No. 175, winter 1992, pp. 12–15
Heinz Isler: Schalen, Katalog zur Ausstellung, Karl Krämer Verlag, 1989
David Billington, The Tower and the Bridge, 1983

Acoustic wall

Gatwick Airport 1998

Structural engineer   **Anthony Hunt Associates**

Client   **BAA**

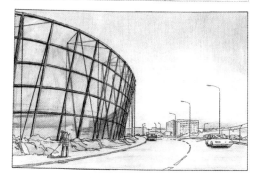

One condition attached to the planning consent given for a new terminal building and associated aircraft stands was that the client should provide an acoustic wall 11 metres high and over 400 metres long to protect adjacent buildings and access roads. At the eastern end the wall would also have to withstand blast from the engines of manoeuvring aircraft.

The entry by AHA to the design competition comprised several alternatives using different materials and structural rationale. Their entry won, not only on the strength of the concept designs, but also on the approach adopted in arriving at them. They considered not only the visual impact and the required acoustic performance, but also details of the construction methods that would be vital to ensure the structure could be built with minimum disturbance to the airport. At every stage of the design development,

great attention was given to matters of minute detail to ensure that little or no finishing treatment to the concrete was needed – a task for which the engineers were able to draw upon their considerable experience of fair-faced and 'architectural' concrete.

The wall is conceived as a folded plate with a constant wavelength of 10 metres – a size chosen to suit the largest size of pre-cast units that could be carried to the site, in pairs, by road. The sinusoidal form is a highly efficient way of achieving the necessary stability relying, mainly, on the dead weight of the blocks. The amplitude of the wave is generally 1.4 metres but is increased to 2.4 metres at the east end to resist the additional loads from aircraft engines. This amplitude is repeated at the western end to achieve a visual balance. At the transition points, two piers of hybrid blocks were made last of all, by cutting the two

moulds for the blocks of different amplitudes and joining one half from each type.

The hollow concrete blocks, 1375 mm high and 500 mm thick, are stacked in piers, eight blocks high. Each pier is independent of its neighbours, partly to minimise the likelihood of a domino effect should something large hit the wall, and partly to ease construction. Each concrete block was pre-cast on the top surface of the block upon which it would rest in its final location. This ensured a near-perfect fit when the blocks were assembled on site. The joints were made waterproof by 'buttering' the top surfaces of each block with just the thinnest layer of epoxy resin before placement.

Further reading
Concrete, October 1998

Westminster & Chelsea Hospital Roof

1992

Structural engineer   Buro Happold

Architect   Sheppard Robson Limited

Client   North West Thames Regional Health Authority

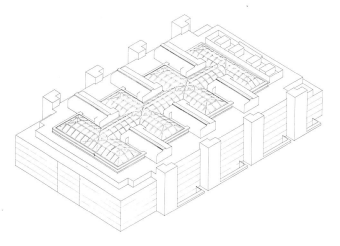

Glass is the usual choice for the transparent material of an atrium roof. However, it is heavy, especially if double glazing is needed to reduce heat losses, and a substantial structure is needed to give a glazed roof sufficient strength and stiffness. This is slightly paradoxical for a building element that is invisible and whose main function, after transparency, is to act as a barrier against heat and rain.

From time to time a project arises in which a variety of factors can suggest to engineer and architect a possible advantage in going back to first principles and analysing an old problem afresh. At the heart of the new Westminster & Chelsea Hospital is a vast barrel-vaulted atrium, 116 metres long and 85 metres wide, with four transepts. In view of the large area to be covered it seemed likely that recent developments in the field of lightweight structures might present some alternatives to the traditional glazing solutions.

The key to good thermal insulation in glazing is the air gap between the glass sheets. Transparent foils of plastic can

also be used to contain the air and are very much lighter but, alone, such a combination of materials has no useful structural properties. Here a lesson was drawn from the field of pneumatic structures: by inflating a flexible sheet it can be prestressed, and the combination of a tensioned sheet and compressed air can produce a structure with some useful rigidity.

These ideas were judged to be worth developing for this large atrium roof, especially in view of the high insulation that might be achieved. A transparent foil of the polymer ethylene tetra-fluoroethylene (ETFE) was found which had adequate tensile strength and resistance to tearing. To increase the thermal insulation it was decided to use three foils and it proved viable to create flat cushions of different shapes by clamping the foils at their edges and keeping them inflated by air maintained at slightly (0.5 per cent) above atmospheric pressure.

The size of the cushions was dictated by their ability to withstand wind and snow loads. The latter would be particu-

larly onerous, and if large panel sizes were to be achieved it became clear that an additional structural system would be needed. This took the form of a series of parallel stainless-steel wires beneath the cushions at 300-mm spacings, which would limit deflections under high loads and provide an additional load path back to the cushion supports. For easy construction it would also be necessary for the cushions to be pre-assembled as self-contained units which could be carried into position and fixed from the outside. The cushions that were developed in this way are about 4 metres x 3 metres in area and 250 mm thick at their centre. They have a thermal performance and transparency similar to triple glazing but at about one fiftieth of the weight.

The very low weight offers enormous potential to achieve both lightness and economy in the supporting structure. Both glass-reinforced plastic and aluminium alloy were considered as materials for making the arched supporting frames, and both have very much better strength-to-weight and stiffness-to-weight ratios than steel. Although the aluminium alternative was finally chosen for its low maintenance needs and superior durability, it also has a particular manufacturing advantage. Aluminium alloys can be formed into extremely complex cross-sections by extrusion through a die. This production technique enabled the many different functions of both the supporting frame for the foil cushions and the structural ribs of the barrel vault to be achieved using just two

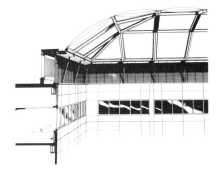

different extruded sections. The requirements were that the frame and ribs should:

- have a high section stiffness (second moment of area);
- support the stainless-steel wire grid;
- allow watertight fixing of the cushion foils into their frame;
- house the air-supply duct needed to inflate the foil cushions;
- incorporate an external gutter for rainwater;
- provide drainage channels for condensation forming in the box section;
- provide small drainage channels to catch condensation forming on the underside of the cushions;
- provide brackets for bolting together the various components and achieving waterproof joints;
- incorporate hooking points for internal cleaning gantries.

The new roofing system thus developed was not produced by taking an existing system and improving individual parts. There was a fundamental rethink as to how to achieve the required performance of an atrium roof. The result is a remarkably tight integration of structure and services: no one part can be changed without affecting some or all of the others – a singular solution for a unique set of circumstances.

It is interesting to note that the principles and logic behind this roofing system – developed by a very 20th-century approach to design and technology – are virtually identical to Paxton's glazed ridge-and-valley system which he developed for the Crystal Palace roof (except for the pneumatic element). But it is in the nature of any innovation, then, as now, that it is not possible to predict at the beginning of a project what the most suitable design will turn out to be. On this project, considerable time and effort for design development was needed in the early stages to achieve an original solution which would finally bring substantial benefits compared with conventional roofing systems. The risk in such an investment in resources is inversely proportional to the level of confidence in the skills of the design team.

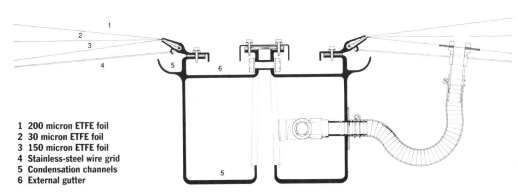

1 200 micron ETFE foil
2 30 micron ETFE foil
3 150 micron ETFE foil
4 Stainless-steel wire grid
5 Condensation channels
6 External gutter

Further reading

Structural Engineering International, Vol. 4 No. 1, February 1994, pp. 14–16

Presbyterian/Korean Church

New York 1999

Structural engineer	Buro Happold	Architect	Garofalo Architects, Greg Lynn, FORM
			Michael McInturf Architects
		Client	Presbyterian Church of New York

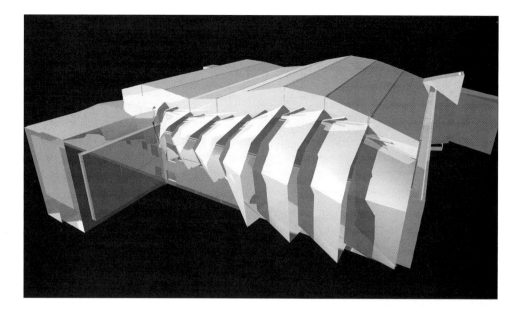

New York, like most cities, has a vast residue of commercial and industrial buildings from former ages that have finally come to the end of their original use. Although such buildings are usually still structurally sound, it poses a challenge to design teams to respect and exploit what is there, while transforming the building to suit a new use and give it a new image. This was the opportunity that presented itself when the Korean community of New York sought to create a new place of worship from a simple, box-like, two-storey, steel-frame building that had housed the Knickerbocker Laundry Factory in the 1930s.

The main challenge was to find a way of providing a sanctuary with seating for up to 2500 worshippers in a building with a regular column grid and 3-metre ceiling heights. Initial ideas had supposed removing part of the first floor and its supporting columns but this left little space for other needs.

The key to the solution was found, literally, by thinking outside the box and using the existing roof as the floor to a second storey. The engineers found that the roof could be made to carry the 2500 worshippers' seats by strengthening the steel beams and replacing the existing concrete slab by a new slab working compositely with the beams. However, placing the worshippers at second-floor level created the problem of providing access and fire exits. The sanctuary would have to be reached by new wide flights of steps and circulation paths which bore little relation to the existing geometry or structural grid. In such circumstances, it is common to use a complex transfer structure to create new

load paths around existing columns that have to be removed; but this would have been too expensive in this community project. A low-tech solution was called for.

Starting from the ground floor, the walls would be built up to the underside of the steel beams and concrete floor, and dry-packed in order to carry the load imposed from above. The superfluous original structure could then be cut away to create the new voids.

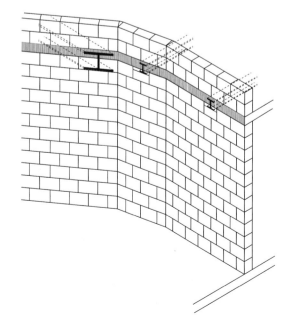

Achieving the simplicity of this solution was made much easier by using a state-of-the-art 3D geometric modelling package used in the automobile industry. This enabled the architects to sculpt the complex voids they proposed for the building. The engineers were then quickly able to assess the structural implications. This dialogue, conducted electronically across many hundreds of miles in the USA, enabled the design team to explore many more possible designs than would have been possible with conventional drawings or models.

The electronic dialogue between architect and engineer also helped in developing the form of the main roof. It was constructed as an essentially independent structure and 'dropped through' the existing building to cover the sanctuary area and the mezzanine which provides additional seating at the rear of the sanctuary. The form of the roof derived from acoustical concerns, reflecting the shape of the ceiling beneath. In order to make the whole structure easier and hence quicker and

cheaper to construct, the engineers took a number of strategic decisions:

- the roof form would be faceted rather than curved;
- the main steel trusses supporting the roof would be of constant depth and horizontal and the roof form would be created by varying the heights of the columns;
- the column spacings would be varied so that the roof joists between them would be of constant length.

The third main element of the building is the grand stair which doubles as an emergency exit and viewing platform. It, too, was devised by thinking 'outside the box' and constructing it on to the north side of the original building. The complex steel frame continues, and makes visible from outside, the forms of the sanctuary's ceiling. The rigid bents that comprise it were described for the fabricators using a 3D model and an extensive set of work-points, resulting in remarkably few fabrication errors despite their complexity. The series of bents is stabilised longitudinally with diaphragms constructed from light-gauge steel joists and plywood panels clad outside in metal and inside in redwood. These diaphragms are warped out of plane owing to the bents' geometry, but the materials used accommodated this without difficulty.

The result is a building of high value to the client, with complex geometry achieved by using software to handle the complexity and to generate the geometry using relatively simple, low-tech structural engineering techniques.

Further reading

Architecture, October 1999

New York Times, 5 September 1999

Aviary

Hong Kong Park

Hong Kong 1991

Structural engineers	Brian Forster, Alistair Day, John White	Architect	Wong Tung & Partners
	Ove Arup & Partners	Client	Royal Hong Kong Jockey Club

In most buildings – from compression structures such as masonry cathedrals to modern braced frames – it is the notional (invisible) line of thrust which moves in response to imposed loads to suit a certain equilibrium state. Actual movements of the structure, needed to develop the forces that resist imposed loads, are relatively small.

Among the types of structure normally used in buildings, tension structures are unique in that in order to establish their state of statical equilibrium, they find their own shape and in doing so may need to move by a relatively large amount. Anyone who has hung washing on a clothes line will have observed this.

Tension structures such as cable nets and fabric tent structures are also characterised by being prestressed; the net or fabric needs to be held taut by forces locked into the structure to give the surfaces some resistance to flapping in wind.

There are two important consequences of these properties of tension structures. The first is that the geometry of such a structure will change significantly during construction as it is hung in position and gradually tensioned to the required level of prestress. The second is that it is essential to be able to predict the <u>final</u> geometry of the structure before it is built in order that cables, nets, panels or fabrics can be cut to precise sizes without the need for thousands of adjustable connectors or guy ropes in an otherwise lightweight, even diaphanous, structure.

It is for these reasons that the computer has been so invaluable to the designers of modern tension structures such as sports stadia and aviaries. Previously, physical models had to be used, but it is no easy matter to make small models which faithfully reproduce the material and structural characteristics of full-size components. It is even more difficult to scale up measurements made on 1:50 or 1:100 models to make full-size components to an accuracy of a few millimetres.

The principle of the Hong Kong Park Aviary is simple: a light, bird-proof mesh hung from a cable net pulled down over three tubular steel arches. The detail was more complex. It was a delicate matter to balance the relative stiffnesses of arch and cable net. The arch supports

the cable net and the cable net stabilises the arch to prevent buckling; however, the thinner the arch, the stiffer the net must be to provide the restraint necessary to inhibit buckling. On the other hand, the thicker the arch, the stiffer it is and the greater the load it attracts and, hence, the sturdier it needs to be.

The site chosen for the aviary presented additional problems – it is in a wooded, steep-sided and meandering valley. Establishing the ground geometry was a difficult enough task, in addition there was the problem of how to represent the geometry of the boundary wall of the cable net as a mathematical

model in a structural analysis computer program. This extremely complex geometrical problem was solved by feeding the data from the site survey into a program more normally used for planning the route of roads through undulating landscapes. It is no exaggeration to say that this would have been impossible to achieve to the required degree of accuracy in the time available using manual calculations. Although computers have gained the reputation of being able to solve many and complex equations in structural and stress analysis, it is easy to overlook the benefit they have contributed by being able to perform (merely!) intricate geometrical calculations.

With the geometry of the cable-net boundary in the computer, the final geometry of the surface was established by performing the computer equivalent of pulling, little by little, an elastic net over the steel arches down to the boundary wall.

From this model could be calculated with precision the lengths of the cables and the angles at which they would have to be joined to one another, the arches

Haj Terminal

King Abdul Aziz International Airport

Jeddah 1980

Structural engineer	**Skidmore, Owings & Merrill**
Services engineer	**Skidmore, Owings & Merrill**
Architect	**Skidmore, Owings & Merrill**
Client	**Ministry of Defence and Aviation**

The terminal building at Jeddah is truly enormous. It needs to provide shelter for up to 80,000 pilgrims at a time – 1.5 million a year – waiting for periods of up to 36 hours, on their way to and from the holy city of Makkah. It covers an area of some 4.25 hectares and even today is still the largest fabric roof in existence.

Since the building is so large (note the relative size of the jumbo jets), ventilation had to be achieved mainly using natural convection. The conical shape of the tensile fabric roof structures was exploited to act as the means by which an updraught could be created. The structure itself thus became part of the services engineering. In addition to the natural stack effect of a chimney, cross winds blowing over the open top of the cones draws air up from below by virtue of lower pressure in the moving air. The precise shape of the roofs was developed after much testing of models in wind- and smoke-tunnels as well as the mod-

elling needed to determine a suitable shape from the structural point of view.

Rather surprisingly, the smoke-tunnel tests and analysis of air-flows and temperatures revealed that the air would be hotter near the ground than immediately beneath the roof fabric. Nine-metre tall ventilation columns were designed to create a forced-air circulation within the building itself. These take the cooler air from above and deliver it down to ground level. The columns were further exploited as multi-service units, housing both the up-lighting and the public-address system.

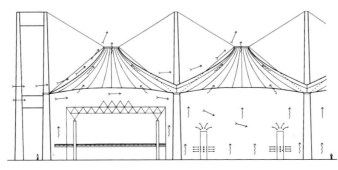

Further reading

<u>Civil Engineering</u> (ACSE), Vol. 50
No. 12, December 1980, pp. 68–71

Royal Court Theatre

London, 1999

Structural engineer Price & Myers

Architect Haworth Tompkins Architects

Client The English Stage Company

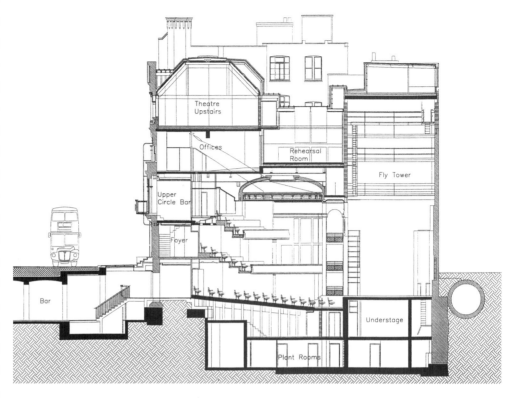

Success, the increasing quality of facilities demanded by audiences, and the requirements of modern theatre and alternative directors can put unexpected pressures on the buildings of old theatres. The original Royal Court Theatre opened in 1888 and by 1903 had already been extended with a second theatre, the Theatre Upstairs. Closed during the Second World War and a cinema in the 1950s, the Court was eventually extended again and refurbished in the early 1980s. Facilities for audiences were improved and a rehearsal room was added in the space above the dome. However, if the theatre was to have a long-term viable future on its existing site, a major overhaul would be required. More space for plant, storage, administration and entertaining would be required, as well as a modern, flexible performance space with all of its associated infrastructure.

In the opinion of the consulting engineers who studied preliminary proposals for introducing the additional space, it would have needed more intervention into the existing structure than would be acceptable out of respect for the original building. While client and architect sympathised with this view, their

choice was stark – unless something was done, the theatre would have to close. The design team from Price & Myers were appointed to devise a means of making the proposals work while, of course, interfering with the existing structure and building fabric as little as possible.

The 1903 and 1985 work had been achieved by carrying the new loads on the original structure, which comprised wrought-iron beams, masonry walls and cast-iron columns. It was soon established that this structure would not be able to carry any more loads. A thorough investigation of how the structure was working or, rather, probably working, revealed several ingenious structural devices – not an uncommon occurrence when investigating old buildings. Most remarkable, given its age, was the con-

scious use of three-dimensional folded-plate action in the horse-shoe shaped, wrought-iron balcony spanning the full width of the auditorium, a span of some 9.5 m. This was, in turn, restrained from twisting by horizontal iron struts carrying the load back to a vertical iron plate embedded in the brickwork of the wall. Understanding such devices is vital to

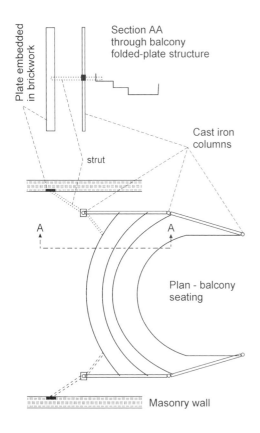

Section AA
through balcony
folded-plate structure

Plate embedded in brickwork

strut

Cast iron columns

A — A

Plan - balcony seating

Masonry wall

Fragile plaster dome
originally supported
by two hangers and
two columns

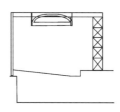

Dome hung from
new beam with
extension.
Supported by two
new columns (left)
and scaffolding in
fly tower (right)

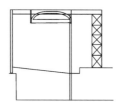

New, longer columns
inserted to support
new beam and dome

Scaffolding support
and extension to
new beam removed

(level 3) as well as the original dome of the auditorium.

There was, however, a problem. The structure supporting the dome would have to be removed before the new column could be inserted to carry the beam that would finally support the dome. At this point in the story, there needs to be a pause to represent the many hours of deliberation, spread over several weeks, about how to break this vicious circle. And, as so often in engineering design, the solution devised is an obvious one – but only with the benefit of hindsight. A 5-metre extension to the new beams would be bolted on and supported on the temporary works structure that would be needed for works in the fly tower above the stage. Once the new columns were in place, and supporting the beam, the extensions were simply unbolted and removed.

minimising the intervention in old buildings during restoration. Here it gave the design team the confidence to leave untouched the original structure of the seating balconies, as long as all the loads from above – including the loads imposed by the 1903 and 1985 additions – could be carried to foundations by a new, independent structural system.

A scheme was devised whereby just four new columns on new foundations would be needed – a pair either side of the proscenium and a pair in the wall at the rear of the auditorium. Two deep box beams – each comprising a pair of 686 mm x 254 mm Universal beams – spanning between the front and rear columns would provide support for the existing Theatre Upstairs (level 4), the new offices and rehearsal space

Given today's commercial pressures on the performing arts a newspaper headline such as 'Engineers save London theatre from closure' would be no exaggeration in this case. The public now sees the original heart of a Victorian theatre served from above, behind and below by the modern facilities needed to keep it alive.

Halley Research Station

No. 4, Brunt Ice Shelf, Antarctica

1983

Structural engineer   Mark Whitby

Anthony Hunt Associates

Timber contractor   Structaply Limited

Architect   Angus Jamieson Associates

Client   British Antarctic Survey

Few buildings travel a distance of 6 kilometres during their useful life; even fewer undertake such a journey underground. In just about every way, a building in the Antarctic is different from what we are all used to. In being so isolated it resembles a space station: from the outset it was known that this building would be totally covered by snow in just a few months; the ice shelf, which floats on the sea, is effectively the end of a glacier and moves about 900 metres each year; materials (except snow) would have to be brought in by ship; construction would have to be completed during the period (72 days) when a ship was able to get to the ice shelf, but during that time work could continue 24 hours a day under the midnight sun.

There has been a British Antarctic Survey research station here since 1956 and the three previous buildings have provided the Survey with invaluable experience in how to design for such an environment. The first building was a timber shed with a substantial roof truss and central column to support the snow that would soon accumulate. It was used for 11 years until 14 metres of snow crushed it. The second building was a steel portal frame, which failed in the same manner after seven years when it was 10 metres beneath the surface.

The third building took note of the similarity between the loads it would suffer and those experienced by a tunnel or submerged tube. An Armco corrugated steel tube, of the type often used to form culverts under roads, resting on a timber raft foundation, acted as a protective cocoon for a non-load-bearing prefabricated timber building. It failed at a depth of 16 metres after 12 years when the bottom of the tube was pushed up by the snow pressures – being a larger radius, the bottom was the weak point in resisting all-round pressure.

Halley 1   Halley 2   Halley 3   Halley 4

Following this failure it was a natural step to consider a circular protective tube for the next research station, Halley 4. In addressing the building's construction, the main challenge was to devise a means whereby its components could be transported and erected easily, and provide adequate structural performance both when newly built and in later life. Immediately after construction it would be at its most vulnerable – a flexible tube resting on a flat surface tends to want to sag and form an oval cross-section; after an Antarctic winter it would be covered by a few metres of snow and would behave as a thin-walled tube.

The design engineer's first step in a project is to develop an adequate understanding of the likely loads on a structure and the properties of the material so that mathematical models can be created to try to predict real structural behaviour. In this case there was little information available, either about loads on buildings buried under snow, or the structural properties of snow itself. The key facts to emerge were that the strength of the snow depended very much on its density and temperature, particularly in the ranges likely to be experienced in the vicinity of the building (450–750 kg/m^3 and between –5 and –18°C).

Structaply worked together with the design engineers to develop a prefabricated timber module that could be assembled, rather in the manner of a Chinese interlocking wooden puzzle, to form a tube which would be resistant

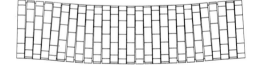

enough to bending to stand alone until covered by snow. The tendency to collapse under its own weight was reduced by excavating a foundation in the snow to support about a quarter of the tube's

circumference (three segments). In addition, snow was heaped and packed up against the walls to give extra support to another segment on each side.

The interlocking segments were held in place during construction by nails, but were designed to be able to articulate to allow the tube to flex under the action of varying loads and differential settlements of the building as it was buried and travelled in the snow towards the open sea.

The accommodation hut sits inside the segmented tube on longitudinal plywood box beams which are located at the points on the tube's cross section which

move least when it deforms into an oval. Initially these beams were fixed to the tube segments to help keep the tube straight. After two years they were disconnected to allow the segments to flex and adapt to the surroundings.

The building survived for ten years until 1992, rather less than fifteen years intended. The need to make the segments easy to assemble left the freestanding building a little too flexible and the tube sagged a little too much during its life before being covered by snow. The result was that the tube was slightly flattened and not able to develop its full strength when acting as a tunnel.

Another unanticipated phenomenon further aggravated this problem. Air was able to reach the snow at the sides of the tube and cause it to sublimate. This created small voids and prevented the snow developing its full lateral pressure on the tube which was so essential to the its stability.

The measurements of the building's geometry taken during its occupation will be useful when designing in similar conditions. With hindsight, perhaps the tube should have been slightly oval in the vertical axis and buried more deeply at the beginning. In fact, Halley Research Station No. 5 has a different design philosophy – it resembles a massive, well-insulated Portakabin and is jacked up by about a metre each year on its twenty legs.

Further reading

Proceedings of 1991 International Timber Engineering Conference, London, TRADA, Vol. 2, pp. 109–118

Tree House

Stoke Pero, Somerset 1979

Structural engineer   <u>Price & Myers</u>

Architect   <u>Beaver Associates</u>

Client   <u>Chris Beaver</u>

The architect wanted to build a tree house for his children, but the only trees available were pines which do not have suitable branches. His first proposal was that the house should span between two trees, on a single beam supported by steel hoops around each trunk and stabilised by struts. The loading would be wind and three children jumping. A dialogue developed.

The engineer suggested using parallel twin beams either side of the tree trunks. A single bolt through the beams and the trunk would form a joint which would both support the house and resist overturning loads due to the wind. The entire house would then be supported at only two points and stabilising struts could be avoided. Also, by bolting the beams together through the trunks, the hoops would not be needed and chafing damage to the bark could be virtually eliminated.

Then there was the question of relative movement between the two trees during a gale. To restrain such movements large loads would have to be carried through the tree house and this would need additional structural material; but these loads could be avoided almost entirely by allowing some relative movement between the trees rather than trying to prevent it. This was achieved simply by elongating the bolt-hole through the beams at one of the tree house's two supports to allow up to 150 mm of longitudinal movement; the bolt bears on PTFE-bearing strips in the slots.

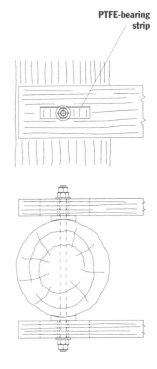

PTFE-bearing strip

Creating value for the client

In Britain we have created a problem for ourselves in separating the design activity from the responsibility for the costs of buildings, which is generally taken by quantity surveyors. However, this does not mean that structural engineers have a reckless attitude to the client's money. Far from it; their whole approach to using materials and designing structures is to use as little material as possible – indeed minimum weight structures are the aspiration of much optimisation in structural design.

However, as our capacity to calculate more and more about structural behaviour has grown, many engineers have lost sight of the bigger picture. It can, for instance, often be cheaper for the client if the sizes and connections of floor beams and columns are limited to just a few alternatives – the benefits of repetition can outweigh the saving in material were each component designed down to its minimum size. It is not more difficult to design in this way; it is all a question of identifying the ultimate goal that the designer is aiming at. The skill of good engineers is apparent in the way they achieve such economy and efficiency without compromising, indeed often by enhancing, the quality of the architecture.

Even this broadening of the engineer's vision, however, is only part of the story. The client is interested in the cost of a building, but is even more concerned with its value – its commercial value, its value to his or her business, its marketing value. Engineers have tended to remain obsessed by costs and how to reduce them, with the result they are often having to work longer and harder now to keep pace with their earnings of ten or twenty years ago. This is devaluing the contribution that engineers make to buildings. But the tide is, perhaps, beginning to turn. Some engineers are focusing more clearly on the value of their work to the client – the value their work can generate for the client. Here is where the future of engineering consultancy lies – in earning larger fees from the large difference between the value and the cost of engineering work to the client.

Increasingly, the idea of value-for-money is embracing not only capital costs, but the performance of a building during its whole life: the costs of running a building, refurbishment, change of use and finally, perhaps, demolition. Just as the reliability and fuel consumption of car or aircraft engines are improved by good engineering design, so too the efficiency of today's high-performance buildings. All this too now needs to be incorporated within the engineer's vision.

The engineering block at De Montfort University began life as the quest for a very low-energy building, which it is. But it has become much more. It is an icon and has been very valuable in marketing the university, to both prospective students and funders of research. The creation of a distinctive identity was also at the front of the client's mind at the Oasis Leisure Village where the hyperbolic paraboloid roof creates a distinct image that now forms a central part of their advertising and marketing.

Sometimes it is the creation of a piece of striking or elegant architecture that best serves the client. The bus station at Chur in Switzerland is an interchange with the railway station and a depot for the lead client, the Swiss postal service. Their public image is important and is enhanced by means of well-designed buildings. The new building at St John's College Oxford serves also to convey the college's values – of high quality and durability. Although more expensive than necessary in terms of capital cost, it will more than repay this in terms of its value to the college, both from the publicity it has brought and the full life-cycle cost spread over 200 years or more.

Often the value to the client is, of course, purely commercial. Ingenious engineering enabled the clients at Queensberry House and Bracken House to gain an entire extra floor to their buildings within the strict height restrictions in London. At the Royal Life Headquarters in Peterborough the design engineers managed to rest their building on a very weak layer of rock in the ground by reducing the weight of the building to less than half that of the first scheme. The saving of many hundreds of thousands of pounds in the foundations enabled the client to spend much more money on the fit-out than had been expected, providing him with much higher quality building. Equally ingenious engineering was used at the Blue Boar development in Cambridge where a large part of the scheme could simply not have been built had not a sufficiently lightweight building been devised which could rest upon the existing supermarket beneath, whose owner permitted the development only on the condition that the supermarket would not be altered, visited or disturbed in any way whatsoever.

School of Engineering and Manufacture

De Montfort University, Leicester 1993

Structural engineer **Martin Cranidge**
YRM–Anthony Hunt Associates

Services engineer **Edith Blennerhassett,**
Max Fordham Associates

Architect **Short Ford & Associates**

In a world where commercial buildings are often marketed on the strength of their performance, rather like cars, it is scarcely surprising that there is a perception that 'more is better'. Consequently, we have arrived at the lunatic position where many floors in buildings are capable of supporting loads three or four times larger than it is possible to place upon them, and air conditioning has become ubiquitous in a climate that hardly ever needs it. In the case of air conditioning the story has been aggravated by the fact that consultants and contractors clearly earn more money if there is more equipment to design and install.

The clients for the new School of Engineering and Manufacture wanted an innovative building, and this would not have been possible with traditional attitudes to building design and procurement. They wanted to create a building which would display the state of the art in environmental awareness, making the best use of natural heating, ventilation and lighting, and traditional construction materials. This required a radical approach to design by the architect and the services and structural engineers – especially the services design consultant who would, in effect, be paid to exclude as many services installations as possible; hardly an approach which a specialist contractor would take. By investing money at the design stage the client has obtained a low-cost building with particularly low running costs.

While the principles behind the design of the building are the same as

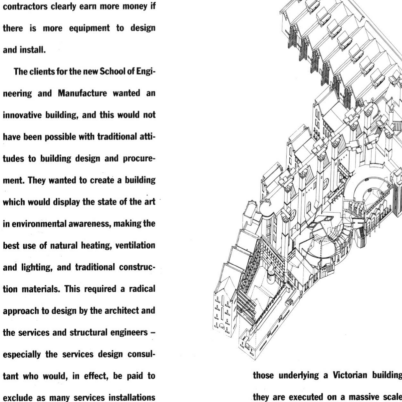

those underlying a Victorian building, they are executed on a massive scale. This required a late-20th-century understanding of the interaction between structure and services – complex three-dimensional load paths, the reinforcement of highly fenestrated masonry façades, differential movements between many materials, air flow

through purpose-designed voids in the structure, and the thermal performance of structural materials. Most particularly, the building design arises not from using a certain sort of structure, or method of servicing or materials technology, but from an attitude to the entire design by every person involved. The philosophy of environmental awareness permeates every aspect of the building, down, almost literally, to the last brick, nut and bolt or pane of glass, and to every area and volume of solid and void throughout an extremely complex three-dimensional geometry. A few examples can hardly do justice to the comprehensive originality of this building.

The design of the building is influenced mainly by the requirements for ventilation and cooling – in many areas the occupants and equipment generate sufficient heat to warm the building, even in winter. The structural and services systems are combined and work entirely passively.

Airflow through the deep-plan parts of the building is generated by the stack effect, a principle well tried in domestic chimneys and in many Arabic buildings in hot climates – warm air at the top of a ventilation duct rises and draws air in at the bottom. In summer the process works on a 24-hour cycle: during the day people and equipment heat the air which then rises up the ventilation ducts. This flow is improved by the design of the exposed tops of the ducts, which are covered with materials to absorb heat from the sun and encourage the stack effect. The ducts are also designed to exploit any cross-winds by channelling the wind to reduce the static air pressure and so draw air up the stack (the effect Bunsen used in his burner). Also, during the day, some of the heat generated within the building is removed as it heats up the fabric of the building. At night the process is reversed. Warm air continues to cycle through the building, drawing in the cool night air over the warm building fabric and removing the heat stored therein. This heat exchange is precisely controlled by regulating the airflow to pre-cool the building just enough to balance the temperature rise it will experience on the following day.

For this system to work it was essential that the materials used for the building structure would absorb sufficient heat and that good heat exchange between the structure and air would be achieved. A great many detailed studies were done to investigate the thermal performance of different designs and to

establish just what airflows and thermal mass the structure would need to discharge its function as a thermal moderator. The result is a large amount of exposed brick and blockwork for walls, and exposed ceilings of either precast-, prestressed-concrete double-T beams or in-situ slabs.

The ventilation ducts are themselves of load-bearing brickwork and are integral to the rest of the building structure. Since they are not needed right down to

ground-floor level, additional useful space was created by supporting them on single, steel columns which branch to support each corner of the diamond- or rectangular-section ducts.

The external walls are perforated by various air intakes to establish precisely the required airflow through the building. As well as having to be integrated into the structure and façade, the intakes needed an acoustic lining to prevent too much noise entering the building – and steel mesh to keep most of the wildlife out.

The walls of the double-height mechanical laboratory needed more substantial lateral restraint than normal because they support a travelling crane. The brickwork structures which buttress the wall are unusual in that they are hollow and act as air ducts. Part of their face is perforated to serve as the air intake.

The ventilation of the circular toilet

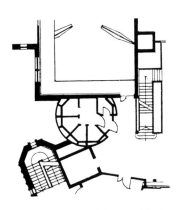

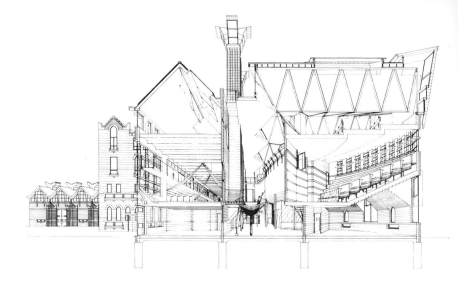

stacks at either end of the central block is on a smaller scale. Independent ventilation is provided from each WC on each floor up to roof level through ducts formed by the void of the double-skin masonry wall.

The requirement for natural daylight also had a direct impact on the structure – large areas of window are needed, often leaving too little masonry to be stable. In the electrical laboratory the load-bearing blockwork had to be reinforced with rods rather like reinforced concrete. Additional stability was pro-

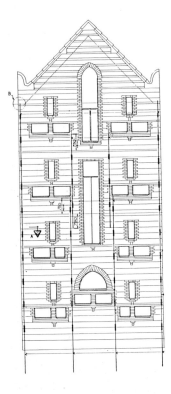

vided around highly-stressed openings by flat reinforcement in the joints between courses of blockwork.

At several places in the buildings daylight is brought through large holes in floors or internal load-bearing walls of upper storeys to illuminate the interior of large ground-floor spaces. In the general laboratory space, for instance, daylight and extract-ventilation is provided by holes so large their edges need their own support. Cranked struts were used to avoid an access walkway and the cruciform sections are fabricated from steel. Their varying cross-section reflects the bending they must resist; they are stabilised by light ties between their knees. The slender, brickwork mullions in the double-storey windows of this room are strengthened by vertical fish-belly Vierendeel girders.

With so many inter-penetrating volumes, both on plan and section, it was not always easy to achieve direct load paths through the building, or to provide enough shear walls to ensure adequate stability. In both the electrical and mechanical laboratories, stability is provided by the end walls, and wind loads are conducted to them through the pitched roofs. These are formed by two in-plane Warren trusses, joined along

their edges so that they can work by folded-plate action.

In the central building the complex internal geometry and lack of a convenient core prevented such a straightforward means of providing stability.

Shear walls shown by double lines

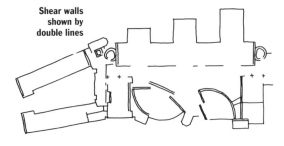

Sufficient resistance to shear had to be provided by a large number of flat and curved vertical surfaces, tied together by the floor screeds and the in-situ-concrete raked floors of the two main auditoria.

The net result is a highly innovative, low-energy building in which, at nearly every turn, the services and structure are working together, often with the same elements serving both systems.

Further reading

Architecture Today, No. 41, September 1993
Building Services, Vol. 15 No. 10, October 1993, pp. 20–25
The Architects' Journal, 9 March 1994, pp. 27–29

Oasis Holiday Village

Near Penrith, Cumbria 1997

Structural engineer <u>Symonds Travers Morgan, David Tasker</u>

Architect <u>Holder Matthias Alcock</u>

Client <u>Oasis Forest Holiday Villages</u>

The client for this project was keen to establish a clear identity for this holiday village to distinguish it from competitors. A circular plan was chosen, with different activity areas arranged around a central core, and it was decided to use the architecture and structure of the roof forms to create individual and distinctive identities to the different zones.

Over the restaurant area, a series of radial laminated-timber arches span 49 metres to provide a visually striking vault, which curves through about 120° of the circular plan. From the warm and robust timber arches spring delicate trusses made of welded steel tubes that,

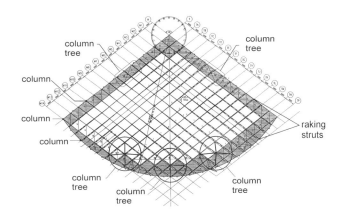

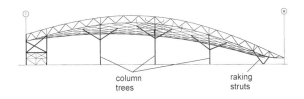

in turn, support the glazed roof.

Over the leisure pool, the challenge was to provide a roof with a strikingly different form while keeping within the client's tight budget and within the low height that the planners required. The plan was also determined – it had to be a 110° sector of a circle, with a radius of 69 metres.

A proprietary space-truss system was proposed but considered rather lacking in character, and its form gave little meaning to the elevation of that part of the building. To be economical it would also need intermediate columns. The project engineer, David Tasker, was

attracted by the possibility of using a hyperbolic paraboloid, not only for its high structural efficiency, but also its form, which is curved in two directions but generated by two series of straight lines intersecting, in this case, at 108°. The curved form is generated by raising one corner of the rhombus out of the plane of the other three. The rhombus is trimmed and built out to fit the circular plan and three perimeter column trees carry the extreme loads from wind uplift

or snow. Being a shell structure, the forces are carried in the plane of the surface and the roof has to carry very little bending – the span is limited only by the need to prevent in-plane buckling.

The complex geometry of the trusses favoured on-site welding and would cost about £10,000 more than the space-truss alternative. However, the client judged that the attractive form and the column-free space would bring to the entire village considerably more value than this higher cost, and so the hyperbolic paraboloid was chosen.

Further reading

<u>Building</u>, 1 March & 15 November 1996

Bus station

Chur, Switzerland 1992

Structural engineer for roof	Peter Rice, Alastair Hughes – Ove Arup & Partners	Consulting engineer	Edy Toscano AG, Hegland & Partner AG
Consultant for glazing	RFR	Architect	Richard Brosi, Robert Obrist
		Lead client	PTT Switzerland

The principal requirement for the roof over the combined bus and rail station at Chur was transparency, both out of respect for the existing 19th-century station buildings and to ensure that the view of the surrounding mountains was not obscured.

A weatherproof and entirely transparent building envelope has been an ideal to strive for since the first large glass walls in Gothic cathedrals. The challenge has always been to reduce the visual impact of the metal supporting structure which any large area of glazing needs. Victorian glass houses undoubtedly got very near the limit, but spans were always small and the imposed loads they had to be designed to withstand were much lower than are required nowadays.

To span 52 metres and at the same time provide a delicate steel structure to give the building stability and enable it to withstand large and possibly asymmetric snow loading, required considerable ingenuity and the full power of modern computer modelling of the structural behaviour. The three-dimen-

sional geometry was often complex and a very high level of accuracy was often essential – all the fixings for the glazing, for instance, had to be positioned to within ±4 mm. To carry out these calculations manually would have been both tedious and labour intensive. Fast computers and three-dimensional CAD soft-

ware were essential to achieve the necessary geometrical accuracy economically; without them the roof and glazing would not have been executed as built.

Each of the twelve 'lemon-slice' (Zitronenschnitz) trusses is formed from a pair of tied, inclined, tubular arches and has a striking visual focus in the cast-steel joint which connects sixteen tie-rods at various angles. The arch tubes are linked by a regular welded grid of tubular purlins which act together effectively to form a Vierendeel lattice or grid shell and give the roof its longitudinal stability.

The decision was taken to keep the glazing and its supporting structure in two separate and parallel planes, linked only by the short radial tubes that support the stainless-steel glazing bars. The contrast between glazing and structure is further emphasised by running the glazing bars only circumferentially; longitudinal joints are of silicone. Above the glazing there is a further layer; thirteen longitudinal rails serve to support the cleaning gantry and to prevent snow sliding down onto hapless pedestrians.

In order to allow good access and circulation at the sides of the building, the roof trusses are suspended in pairs from twin columns, which themselves cantilever from the foundations so that both lateral and longitudinal stability is achieved without the need for cross-bracing.

Being a semi-outdoor building, few services are required, but so sparse is the roof structure that even a few electrical conduits would have impaired its purity. The lighting for the entire bus station ingeniously avoids this problem. Clusters of convex mirrors are suspended high up and lit by spotlights mounted on the columns just above eye-level at the side of the building.

Further reading

Arup Journal, Vol. 28 No. 21, 1993, pp. 3–7
Werk, Bauen + Wohnen, No. 11, November 1993, pp. 28–35

Royal Life Headquarters Building

Peterborough 1991

Structural engineer **Arup Associates**

Architect **Arup Associates**

Client **Royal Life Holdings Limited**

The first schemes for this new headquarters building incorporated a coffered floor slab and represented the natural evolution of a structure and servicing philosophy that the practice had developed over many years in a wide variety of building types. The site chosen for the building was known to be of weak clay and the coffered structure would have required a large number of piles some 20 metres long. This sub-structure would have consumed a significant proportion of the total building costs and construction time.

Often a client will have in mind a certain cost for a new building well before it has been designed. If the chosen site presents unforseen problems below ground, this may simply mean that a larger proportion of the money will be needed for elaborate foundations and this will have to be found by reducing the proportion spent above ground. Conversely, if an ingenious means can be found to reduce foundation costs, the client might then be able to spend more money on the visible parts and get an altogether higher quality of building.

The site investigation confirmed the existence of the weak clay and revealed an unexpected layer of Cornbrash (a cemented sandstone) covering the entire site. It varied in depth from 3 to 6 metres below ground level, was only about 800 mm thick and cracked in a number of places. There was no possibility that this layer could support the proposed building and the 20-metre piles that would have to be driven through it. Spurred on, perhaps, by

thoughts of the cost of this operation, the structural engineer looked at the problem from the other end: what load <u>could</u> the Cornbrash layer support? The answer was a building with a self weight less than half that of the original scheme – a challenge indeed.

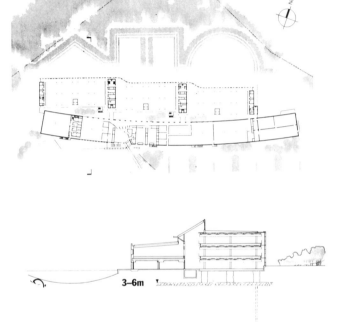

One by one different structural ideas were considered which would reduce the original self weight of about 820 kg/m^2 per square metre. By decreasing the size of the grillage of the coffered floor the weight would be reduced to 760 kg/m^2. A composite in-situ/precast scheme was examined: precast troughs where downstands would be exposed, and just strong enough to support the weight of wet concrete when casting the main floor structure. It would weigh about 630 kg/m^2. A flat slab with raised floor was considered: this would reduce the building height and bring the weight to around 600 kg/m^2. Finally a hybrid

skeleton of in-situ concrete and steel was proposed, with primary beams of concrete in one plane, and secondary beams of steel in another. By this means the height of the building was kept low and a weight of just 365 kg/m^2 was achieved – within the limit of what the Cornbrash layer could support and distribute over a large area of the weaker clay beneath.

One key to the success of the hybrid scheme was the decision to link pairs of concrete frames containing the primary beams – by means of small concrete beams in the plane of the steel secondary structure – to form a series of Vierendeel towers. Their resistance to wind loads is augmented by the steel beam and metal decking floor structure which links and acts compositely with the towers to provide longitudinal stability.

The hybrid construction was inherently quick to build – important to a client who wanted to occupy the building as soon as possible. An all-concrete frame and floor could have started on site quickly but would have taken longer to complete; an all-steel frame and metal decking floor would have been quick to construct but the lead time for the structural steelwork would have meant a long delay before work could start on site. The hybrid scheme allowed the frame to begin immediately and be completed during the lead-in time for the steelwork.

As well as being lighter, the hybrid structure itself was also cheaper – about two thirds of the cost of the earliest scheme; and, of course, the greatest saving was in the cost of the (non-visible) structure below ground. Rather than a forest of long and costly piles, the foundations effectively comprise a grid of short concrete pillars. These serve two purposes: they carry the loads from the building directly down to the Cornbrash rock and spread the load from each column foot over an area large enough to prevent the columns from puncturing the thin rock layer. They would also serve to seal any fissures in the rock and protect the crack edges from potentially damaging load concentrations. The cost of these foundations was kept very low by using the clay above the Cornbrash as the formwork for the pillars. Holes were made using the largest available auger (2 metres diameter) to drill down through the clay to the rock. After cleaning out and inspection

these were immediately filled with concrete without even the need to support the sides of the holes.

Despite the constructional logic behind all these ideas, two important aspects of the original architectural scheme were in danger of being lost – a coffered ceiling and exposed concrete of the quality usually achieved by precasting.

The structural engineer was able to deliver the required high-quality finish to the concrete by contributing to the development of a 'structured formwork' system for use on site which incorporated many of the benefits of precasting techniques. A U-shaped trough 4.5 metres long was made by folding a steel plate to produce corner radii three times smaller (just 8 mm) than the usually-quoted minimum. A series of fins was welded to the plate to prevent distortion and the sides supported by external bracing. The bracing structure incorporates the mechanism which allows the sides to be pulled apart to facilitate removing the formwork; it also supports a walkway for use when placing the reinforcement and concrete, thus reducing the need for access scaffolding. The two sides of the mould are joined by a clamp which serves to restrain the sides during pouring and to support the tie-down bolts for the steel secondary beams.

The floor structure allows flexible distribution of services. Longitudinal runs are beneath a raised floor and large transverse service runs are created by the suspended flat ceiling in the short

bays of the concrete Vierendeel towers. This strategy enabled the services to be installed quickly and cheaply and with a minimum of effort: access to all the services voids was easy and no large holes had to be made through structural members. The final development of the ceiling was to incorporate a suspended vault between the secondary beams in the long bays. This controls both light and acoustic to achieve the required degree of intimacy in the office space.

In summary, while the hybrid scheme began 'merely' as a technical device, its adoption and development made a fundamental contribution to the aesthetic and the architecture of the whole building.

All designs change as they develop, and ingenuity is often stretched when major new ideas appear well into a project. It had originally been intended that the façade of the office building would follow the line of the structural frame where the building steps back at the lift and stair cores. As the design of the glazed screen developed it was decided that the façade should sweep in a curve from one block to the next in order to avoid the abruptness of the sudden change of plane and to reinforce the idea of a screen between the building and the surrounding formal landscape. But this would take the façade some 7 metres away from the frame at two points, at which it would need its own load-bearing structure. Unfortunately, the only steel tube available at such short notice was too small in diameter. Making a virtue out of necessity, the section stiffness of the available tube was increased by welding four pairs of longitudinal fins made from steel of the same section as the aluminium used in the façade structure itself. The result is a striking unity between the different elements of the façade and gives the clear impression of subtle forethought.

Further reading

Concrete Quarterly, No. 172, Spring 1992, pp. 19–21
Architectural Review, May 1992, pp. 44–53
Arup Journal, Vol. 26 No. 3, Autumn 1991, pp. 3–10

Blue Boar Court

Cambridge 1990

Structural engineer
Phil Cooper

Harris & Sutherland

Architect
MacCormac Jamieson Prichard & Wright

Client
Trinity College, Cambridge

Trinity College wished to redevelop an old city-centre hotel site into a fine residential courtyard, gaining some valuable commercial space in the process. On a podium formed by the roof over the existing shops, new and old buildings now form a series of intricate courts linked by bridges, ramps and passages. What is not so obvious is the scarcity of support for these apparently massive, traditional brick and stone buildings. The structural engineer's contribution to design is often discreet -- sometimes, indeed, invisible or deceptive.

Normally the space in which an engineer is free to build is enclosed only by a site boundary. Here the space for development also had to interlock with existing buildings, both above and below. For the architect the design

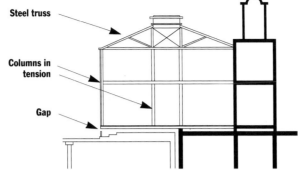

Steel truss

Columns in tension

Gap

became a complex three-dimensional puzzle comprising closely-packed rooms arranged around courtyards. For the engineer the challenge was to construct these buildings, some of which were stranded with no obvious means of structural support.

Although the brick façade of the Common Room exactly matches adjacent load-bearing masonry buildings, it is in fact framed in steel and timber. And this is not the only sleight-of-hand; more than half of the Common Room is cantilevered out over Sainsbury's and Heffers Bookshop and is counterbalanced by the large weight of the adjacent tower

and its basement. Although the columns appear, as one might expect, to support the upper floors and roof, it is the roof that supports the floors, and the 'columns', made of steel tube clad in oak, are actually working in tension.

The 140-seat lecture theatre is built on the roof of Sainsbury's supermarket. Settlement and cracking had to be avoided at any price since access to the interior of the busy supermarket was denied totally. Only four columns were available to carry all the loads from the new theatre down through the supermarket to the raft foundation.

The weight of the paving on the original roof was removed and the weight of the new theatre had to be pared to the bone. Indeed, so nearly did the loads carried by the four columns approach the limit that the process became more like that of designing an aircraft – even the weight of an extra layer of plasterboard for acoustic insulation had to be traded against other more essential loads. Although these columns do now carry larger loads than originally, the design engineers were able to provide adequate justification that there was enough reserve capacity to ensure that safety standards for the public shopping areas below would not be compromised.

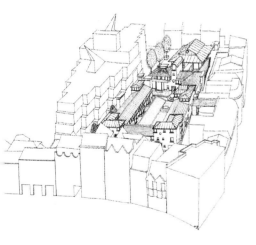

Further reading

The Architects' Journal,
5 December 1990, pp. 32–43 and
48–49

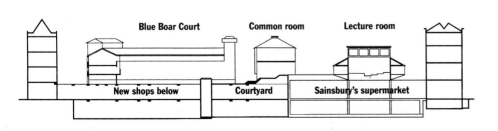

Blue Boar Court   Common room   Lecture room

New shops below   Courtyard   Sainsbury's supermarket

Bracken House

London 1991

Structural engineer   John Thornton, Rob Kinch
                       Ove Arup & Partners

Architect   Michael Hopkins & Partners
Client   Obayashi Europe BV

Bracken House was formerly the head-quarters of the Financial Times. The new building retains the two end wings of the 1959 listed building but replaces the centre with a design rather closer in form to Guarini's Palazzo Carignano which had inspired the original design. No building is conceived in a vacuum, and design concepts pass from one project to another: old ideas and materials are revisited, new combinations are found. In Bracken House several themes used in the Mound Stand at Lord's cricket ground, on which engineers and architect had worked together, are re-used and developed further.

The proximity of St Paul's Cathedral meant severe height restrictions and called for particularly close integration of structure and services in order to reduce the height of each storey to 3.9 metres and so be able to incorporate six floors in the new central section of the building, rather than five. At the same time the architect wanted the façade to be part of the structure rather than a curtain wall.

THE CONCEPT : WHEEL   STRUCTURAL ORGANISATION

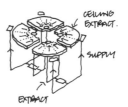

FLOOR SERVICES SUPPLY
BETWEEN STRUCTURE

CEILING EXTRACT.

SUPPLY

EXTRACT

Many different structural schemes were considered in the search for one which would provide a sufficiently thin floor sandwich – in-situ-concrete beams and slabs, precast-concrete beams, steel beams with concrete fire protection and vaulted slabs reminiscent of the brick jack-arches used in many 19th-century industrial buildings.

Inspired partly by the architectural scheme for the building outline, it was decided to impose a radial organisation to the services and structure and ensure that no large services needed to cross the line of the beams. Their lower surface could be left exposed, both to save the space lost above a false ceiling and to express the building's structural and services grid. This idea favoured the choice of precast-concrete beams which, as well as giving the high quality of finish required, would also help increase the speed of construction. The columns are of in-situ concrete.

The main services run in the void between the radial beams. In order to locate the supply air ducts and fans at floor level and the lighting units and

Exploring the unknown: managing risk and delivering confidence

The structural engineer's main contribution to most building projects is to offer a professional guarantee of their safety and fitness for (structural) purpose, in order to provide the client, architect and users of the building the confidence they require. Put another way, it is to reduce to acceptable levels the risks to which these people might be subjected, and to ensure low insurance premiums. Good engineering design, especially the right input at the concept design stage, can not only reduce the risk of collapse or poor structural performance, it can also significantly improve the likelihood that a project will be completed on time, within budget and to the specified quality.

All this is especially true of unusual projects or those that involve significant technological innovation. It is all a matter of confidence. First the engineer has to build up his or her own confidence. This must then be conveyed to others on the project and finally to the client and the public.

Raising confidence in a design may be achieved by many means. It has long been done by making models or full-size prototypes but these are increasingly augmented and sometimes replaced by the use of mathematical models which are nowadays set up to be tested and to 'behave' inside a computer. With the falling cost of powerful computers during the last decade or so, building engineers are able to model much more complex structures and more unusual materials than before. They can also now assess the influence of phenomena which could previously not be modelled at all – phenomena such as the behaviour of structural elements and entire buildings in fires, the dynamic behaviour of buildings in winds and earthquakes, even the behaviour of people fleeing a building in a fire.

In the construction industry it is unfortunate that innovation is seen by many clients as something to avoid at all costs. Engineers frequently remove from their design proposals any mention of the new, for fear of it being prohibited. In fact, clients are benefiting from engineering innovation all the time. Engineers do indeed often deceive their clients by not telling them about new ideas they want to use. However, the problem is more fundamental. In highly technological industries such as the aircraft industry, the 'client' is more technically educated and better able to understand and judge the nature of innovation, as well as the likelihood of it being successful. These clients are therefore much more able than most construction clients to see the benefits they are likely to achieve as a result of innovation. And a substantial reason for this is that structural and other building engineers have been, and are, very poor at demonstrating to clients the nature of those benefits. For a start it is rather ironic, though rather human, that the issue of confidence tends to be addressed and measured according to the likelihood of failure rather than of success – risk analysis rather than success analysis. But this is a methodology taken from the financial world. It is up to engineers to develop their own skills in persuading people of the benefits to be gained from good engineering and using innovative engineers.

At the l'Oréal factory in Paris the design engineer had devised a complex, three-dimensional roof truss which required a bespoke,

cast-steel node that could be adapted to different locations where up to twelve members might join. The complex stress flows through the node were modelled using a computer but it was felt wise to gain greater confidence by testing a full-scale mock-up to validate the mathematical model and to proof test the node to twice its design load. At Minster Court in London a stack of sixteen escalators are suspended from just four points. A careful analysis was undertaken in order to reduce to an acceptable level the risk of problems arising in service from the complex dynamic loading arising from both people and the machinery.

At Trinity College Cambridge an underground store room was to be built adjacent to the famous library by Christopher Wren: the consequences of causing any movement to the foundations of the library were dire and great ingenuity was needed to devise a suitable way of building the new room. At Albert Dock in Liverpool it was an old building itself that was to be restored and great care had to be taken to understand how it was working as a structure before any intervention could be made, or new proposals made. As a result of understanding how the unique roof was working, the engineers were confident that it would need only basic repairs to be serviceable well into the future. An inadequate understanding of this roof would have led a less-skilful engineer to have condemned it and demanded it be replaced.

At Bedfont Lakes near Heathrow Airport, the risk of the building being damaged by fire has been reduced using a fire engineering approach to the design of the building. By modelling the behaviour of the structure in a fire, its safety can be ensured without the need for conventional fire protection which is expensive, time-consuming to install and unsightly. At the new Lloyd's headquarters building in London, the engineers were able to help the client and the contractor to reduce their exposure to commercial risk by devising a structural system in pre-cast concrete so that the frame could be assembled quickly on site, providing the client with the high-quality exposed concrete finishes required without the risk of production problems causing unpredictable delays.

The last project in this chapter inhabits the world of extreme risks and is a striking example of the rewards which engineering innovation can bring. By looking at how to carry the loads imposed by earthquakes with the fresh eyes of an outsider, engineers at Ove Arup and Partners were able to devise an entirely new type of building on the Tokyo skyline with an unprecedented area of windows.

Structural engineer Richard Hough, Mike Banfi

<u>Ove Arup & Partners International</u>

Architect <u>Valode et Pistre et Associés</u>

Client <u>L'Oréal</u>

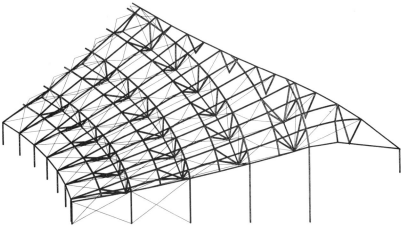

The image chosen for the roof of L'Oréal's new factory was of the petals of a white flower draped over the three clear-span space-frame structures that house the manufacturing areas.

In order to provide an open floor space it was decided to support the roof structure only at its perimeter and, as a consequence, the largest radial spans are around 60 metres. A two-way spanning structure was chosen to minimise its weight. The resulting space-frame comprises a grid of radial V-shaped trusses and circumferential planar trusses and has a simple, homogenous expression which reflects that of the roof panels above. Within the space-frame pattern, inverted square-based pyramids were chosen as key visual elements, seeming to prop the petals with

their sets of four tubular fingers.

The presence of the pyramids in the space-frame geometry is accentuated by maximising the use of tension members in the surrounding structure, leaving the tube pyramids apparently suspended in space. This makes for a rather more subtle structural behaviour than might at first be supposed. Different combinations of the tension members are used to carry the forces arising from the different load conditions which may act on the roof. Since the slender tie-rods cannot carry loads in compression, the computer model of the structure used for studying member forces and deflections had to be non-linear. Thus, as changing loads might reduce the force in a tie to zero, any further change would result in the member effectively disappearing from the model since it cannot carry compression.

Between the scheme design stage and final agreements with the steelwork contractor, wind-tunnel testing was undertaken in order to justify the

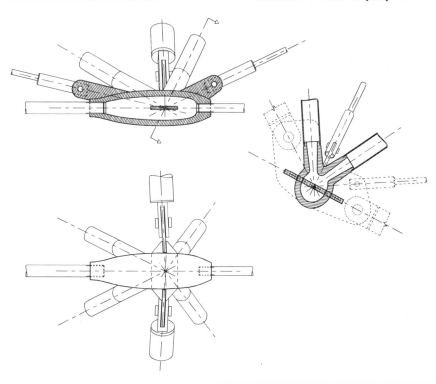

assumptions that had been made about uplift loads on the roof due to the wind. This resulted in a net saving to the client as the reduction in the amount of steel used in the roof more than covered the cost of the tests and additional structural analysis.

Many tubes and rods meet at the apexes of the pyramids. Most of these nodes join the four fingers, two circumferential tubes and six tie-rods at various angles – 12 members in all – and, to prevent rotation, the centre lines of the members must all meet at a single point. This joint is an important visual focus in sculptural terms and its shape was developed to reinforce the structural theme of 'tubes-dominant, ties-recessive'. A steel casting was chosen to bring sufficient mass of steel to the joint to

carry the forces while allowing its form to be sensitively sculpted. The radial tie-rods screw into the casting while other tie-rods are linked by pins to gusset plates welded to its surface. The circumferential tubular members are connected to a plate which passes through the hollow centre of the joint. This allows the wall thickness of the casting, the main body of which is 265 mm in diameter and 850 mm long, to be substantially reduced down to just 32 mm.

For such an unusual component it was judged that theoretical studies alone would not give sufficient justification of its structural behaviour or the magnitude of any stress concentrations within the casting. A trial joint was loaded on a specially-built test rig and gauges were used to measure the strain

in the surface of the casting, especially in likely areas of stress concentration. From these measurements a reliable picture of the flow of stresses within the steel itself was built up; in particular, stress levels at the points of stress concentration were confirmed as meeting the criteria for avoiding local failure due to metal fatigue. The castings were also proved capable of withstanding twice their anticipated service load without suffering permanent deformation.

Further reading

Le moniteur, No. 4652, 22 January 1993
Arup Journal, Vol. 27 No. 3, Autumn 1992, pp. 11–13

Trinity College Book Store

Cambridge 1991

Structural engineer   Peter Leveridge

Harris & Sutherland

Client   **Trinity College, Cambridge**

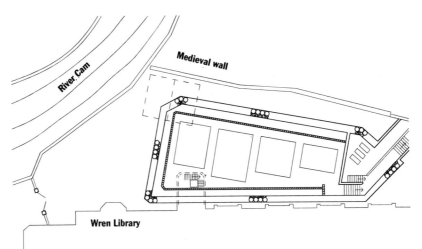

Soil is probably the most challenging material that structural engineers have to deal with. It is not made in factories and its properties can never be known as reliably as those of steel, timber or even concrete. Furthermore, its engineering properties depend utterly on the presence (or absence) of water and whether the soil particles have been disturbed from their natural state – for instance, by excavation.

The urgent need for additional book storage space at Trinity College presented various problems as there were few acceptable possibilities for introducing new buildings into the medieval court. A scheme was proposed for a new store beneath a narrow, enclosed wedge of land by the River Cam, adjacent to Wren's library. This led to a number of engineering challenges: gaining access to the site, ensuring long-term watertightness against a 5-metre head of water, minimising any disturbance to the water-logged soil around the site and, of course, leaving the adjacent structures undamaged. To maximise the space for books, the basement walls had to be placed as close as possible to existing buildings – 300 mm from a Victorian building and 2 metres from a medieval boundary wall of uncertain stability. In order that site traffic did not have to use an 18th-century masonry bridge, access to the site was provided by a Bailey bridge over the River Cam.

Construction of any basement entails the removal of a substantial weight of soil and this leads to a relief of stress on the underlying soil. When relieved of

stress, the clay on this site expands as water enters the pores in the clay. Since this can exert substantial forces on any basement floor it is customary to provide a void beneath a basement into which the heaving clay can expand. This can, however, bring new problems – soil outside the excavation can migrate around the toe of the wall and might, in turn, cause subsidence of adjacent buildings.

To avoid these problems the design engineers decided to construct the building in such a way that the stress condition under the site would be disturbed as little as possible. Thus, not only would the building be literally invis-

ible, being underground, but also even the soil beneath it would hardly be affected by its construction. This was achieved by several means.

The book store takes the form of a box within a box to provide two barriers against water ingress. The outer barrier is of reinforced concrete. Inside, a suspended floor, an inner metal-clad roof and wall panelling will protect the books should any water penetrate the concrete. If necessary the panels can also give access to allow repair of the concrete walls.

The 12-metre secant piles forming the impervious structural retaining wall were formed using a continuous flight auger. In this process the concrete forming the pile is pumped down the centre of the auger, which is gradually forced out of the ground. There is thus never an empty hole which would allow the water and soil to move and hence disturb the equilibrium of the soil. The inward deflection of these piles was monitored continuously during construction so the engineer could be sure that the pressure of soil and water on the wall was not

the concrete planks rest on the protruding plate, the difficulty of inserting planks between the beam flanges was avoided. Shear studs are welded to the top flange of the beam and tied to the reinforcement in the concrete topping in order to achieve fully composite action of the whole floor structure. By this means it was possible to span 6 metres with a steel section just 203 mm deep.

Most of the cross-section of the floor beams was to be embedded in concrete

and fire protection was not an issue. It was decided to protect the exposed surface of the steel plate using fire-board. While design and construction proceeded, British Steel undertook a number of fire tests which demonstrated that the exposed surface would not, in fact, need fire protection. This was later confirmed by a theoretical fire-engineering study involving the computer modelling of the temperature levels and heat flow in the composite section when subjected to a range of plausible fire loads. These results were too late to affect the construction of the IBM building, but the success of the approach has been established and similar composite sections are now being promoted as a highly efficient way of using steel.

As a steel building through and through, two further structural details are worthy of note. Throughout the building the architects wanted the columns to reflect the size of load they

carry and the transition between different sections at different floors is pointed up by an ornate casting. Although thirty differently-shaped castings were originally planned for the entire building, it would have proved too costly to have them all made. Various design details were modified and rationalised so that finally just six different patterns were needed by the foundry. As malleable cast iron cannot be welded satisfactorily, cast steel was chosen. The different nodes and column sections were welded together in the fabrication shop and brought to site as full-height columns.

Steel also plays a part in providing the building with its lateral stability. This is provided not by the usual cross-bracing or concrete shear wall in the building cores, but by steel shear plates in the façade, based on the same module as the cladding. Although vertical fins are apparent, they are for appearance rather than stiffening: at 15 mm thick, in order to avoid visible distortion caused during the cutting and fabrication processes, the plates are more than thick enough to cope with wind loads by acting in tension across their diagonals.

Futher reading

Architectural Review, October 1992, pp. 25–35

Albert Dock

Liverpool 1842–48/1982–88

Structural engineer   **Jesse Hartley**

Curtins Consulting Engineers

Client   **Merseyside Development Corporation**

The 19th century has left Britain with a wonderful legacy of commercial and industrial buildings – warehouses, mills and factories, made of brick or stone combined with cast iron and wrought iron. These materials are very durable and it is a sign of relatively enlightened times that the cry 'if it's old, knock it down', so prevalent in the 1960s and '70s, is heard less often today. There is now no excuse for demolishing buildings that are structurally adequate and which, with a modicum of architectural and engineering skill and sensitivity, can be transformed to suit a range of viable modern uses.

The issue of structural adequacy is, however, a deep subject and one which is all too easily misunderstood. Using a narrow definition – would the building entirely satisfy a modern code of practice? – most 19th-century buildings would probably be condemned; after all, modern codes cater only for modern materials and construction details. At the other extreme, it is clearly unwise to argue simply that if a building is still standing it must be safe. Between these two extremes there are many subtle variations.

The iron structure which supports the masonry vaults of Jesse Hartley's ware-

house buildings on the Liverpool waterfront is unique. The ingenious cross-sections and sculptured forms make it one of the most remarkable examples of the use of cast iron in building. Given this and their imposing site, these dock buildings were clearly worth preserving and are, indeed, Grade I listed.

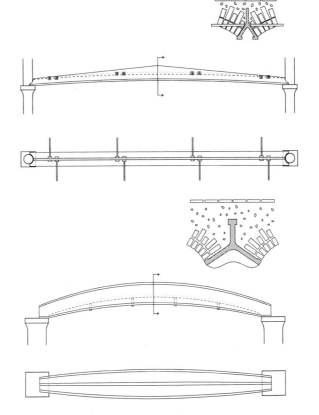

However, although the floors were originally designed to withstand about 15 kN/m^2, an initial assessment of the structure suggested that the adequacy of some of the floors could not be justified using a rigorous application of modern codes. The main reason was that the conservative value for the tensile strength of cast iron, which is generaly recommended, is extremely low. Similar initial conclusions were drawn concerning some of the masonry walls, the integrity of the iron structure, and the piled foundations, none of which would quite satisfy the modern codes. And yet the buildings gave every appearance of being very robust and, despite heavy use, had survived with little distress for nearly 140 years.

An alternative approach was taken and some of the assumptions behind the initial assessment were examined more carefully. For instance, although there was evidence of corrosion, more detailed investigations established that it did not penetrate very deeply beneath the surface; the structural cross-section was thus not as seriously weakened as

Putting structure on show: the engineering aesthetic of materials

Architecture is an act of communication – careful choices by building designers that are intended to evoke feelings and physical sensations in people who see or use the building. Engineers sometimes talk about 'reading a structure'. This too implies a message that is being communicated – an underlying concept or intention which is there for others to see or to interpret. So what do we see when we see a structure? It is much more than mere appearance – their colour and surface texture. We see materials that we know something about. They might be hard, or strong, or warm to the touch, or brittle. And we know even more than this. Indeed, in every aspect of the way a material is used in a structure, the very essence of that material is on show – an essence that goes far deeper than material properties such as strength and stiffness. Deepest of all is how the material gets used – both alone and in combination with other materials – the very means by which it can be shaped, joined and manufactured into useful artefacts. Together all this constitutes the engineering aesthetic of a material, its very soul.

A material cannot be used in the abstract. It must have form and it must be connected to other pieces. Certain structural forms, such as the parabolic or the catenary arch, are imbued with their significance by the underlying laws of nature. Other forms owe their distinction to methods of manufacture such as rolling, extrusion or casting. Methods of connection too have their origin in the exigencies of both statics and manufacturing.

Take cast iron, for instance – and it does matter whether we take Victorian, brittle cast iron or the modern malleable material – its soul is there in the surface texture and shapes made possible by the casting process, the structural forms characteristic of its being used in tension, compression or bending, whether it is being used in conjunction with wrought-iron ties, brick jack-arches or a wrought-iron beam, the means by which it can be connected to other elements, and so on.

Likewise, the soul of timber is there in the dimensions of structural components and the shape of nails and screws which can be driven into it; the soul of glass is there in the details of fixings needed to prevent stress concentrations; the soul of wrought iron is there in the shape of rolled sections and the appearance of a hand-closed rivet; the soul of aluminium is there in the extruded shape of a glazing bar and even in the gaps needed to prevent cold bridging; the soul of concrete is there in the surface pattern from the formwork and the hue of a polished granite aggregate; and the soul of mild steel is there in a forged connector welded to a rolled beam section.

These feelings can be evoked by any use of a material. In the hands of the designer they become part of a deliberate communication process. As Peter Rice said, 'a material is used to express its inner nature with feeling and is clearly the work of a designer who, in thinking about the material, has made the perception of the material more real. ... The search for the authentic character of a material is at the heart of any approach to engineering design.'

In the sports stadium at Montreuil near Paris, Marc Mimram has taken a familiar material, steel, and used it in remarkable new ways. Simply by cutting, folding and welding we see unfamiliar qualities and characteristics of steel, and we see the hand of the computer in making feasible complex geometries that would otherwise be too costly. The material seems to acquire the spirit we see in wrought ironwork, of being crafted by a human. At the new Orangerie in Prague we see the other face of steel – the machine age and mechanical precision reflecting the city's long tradition in those arts.

In the Educatorium at the University of Utrecht we again see a new face to an old material, reinforced concrete. Holland is well advanced in its concern for the environmental impact of buildings and this has given a new significance to the engineer's skill at reducing the amount of material, or rather the amount of embodied energy, used to make a structure. Just as this roof gives the users of the lecture hall a constant reminder of the materials used in construction, so too at Totton Primary School, where laminated timber is used to express to the pupils (future engineers?) the very way the wood is put together and made to work as a structure. And we see the same transparency of purpose in three similar roof trusses which, when considered or read carefully, can be seen to work in slightly different ways betraying the different wind loads acting on the roofs.

In more spectacular fashion, in the glass façade at the London Headquarters of Channel 4, and the granite structure of the Pabellon del Futuro for EXPO '92 in Seville, we see how the materials need to work in partnership with steel because of their own brittleness and methods of manufacture. In a very visible sense, the steel is expressing the brittle character of the glass and the stone.

Montreuil Sports Stadium

near Paris 1993

Structural engineer   **Marc Mimram**

Architect   **Marc Mimram**
Project associate   **Christophe Barthelemy (Architect)**
Client   **Montreuil Town Council**

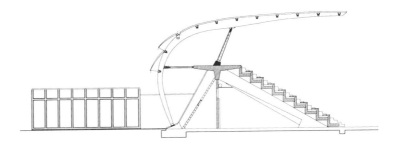

This municipal sports complex comprises three elements: changing facilities, the stand (beneath which are all the common facilities), and a roof to shelter the spectators. All are clearly differentiated, both in location and in the manner of their construction. The changing rooms at the rear are formed by six small and independent metal-clad concrete-wall 'boxes', the stands are built from in-situ reinforced-concrete portals supporting precast-concrete seating, and the roof is supported on ten pairs of curved steel box-girders with varying cross-sections.

Such is the complexity of the form of these sections that it is no exaggeration to say that the building could not have been designed or fabricated at an economic cost without the direct data link between the computer drawings and the computer-controlled cutting and welding equipment. By this means it was possible to create the form of the building elements almost in the manner of a sculptor working directly with the steel.

Although the metal frame which supports the roof contrasts with the con-

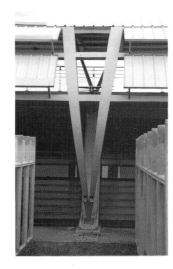

crete portals of the stands, they were nevertheless conceived to form a coherent structure. The two elements are articulated both at their common base and at the foot of the V-shaped struts which support the upper ends of the main roof ribs and provide longitudinal stability.

The roofing itself comprises three skins with distinct functions:

- the centre layer is a galvanised self-stiffened metal sheet and forms the waterproof layer;
- the upper layer of tensioned white aluminium sheets gives the roof a continuous external finish;
- the under side is faced with treated plywood panels which give a unity to the volume of the stand.

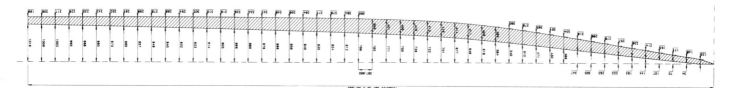

The main curved ribs are manufactured entirely from flat steel plates and fabricated using computer-controlled cutting and welding machinery. This technique is now widely available and can enable a designer to create complex geometric forms such as a continuously variable cross-section and, hence, section stiffness (second moment of area). A steel structure can thus be given a form which faithfully reflects the loads it must carry.

Each curved box-girder rib comprises 13 sections, each of which is bounded by four uniquely curved faces. Since the lines of intersection between these 52 surfaces cannot be defined as parts of simple geometrical curves, it would not have been possible to mark them out with sufficient accuracy on the steel plate prior to cutting. The CAD computer was programmed to calculate the co-ordinates of a large number of points along the edges and feed these directly to the computers controlling the oxy-acetylene cutting tools. The steel plates are joined by a continuous weld in the exposed angle formed where one plate overhangs the other at right-angles.

A similar technique was used to manufacture the V-shaped struts which stabilise the cantilever roof ribs and the horizontal ties between the ribs and concrete stand, both of which help to give shape to the volume that forms the upper promenade of the stand. They, too, feature a varying section, though it was created in a different way. Two steel tubes of different radii were cut longitudinally at an angle and welded together to form a closed section. The connections between the struts and the roof rib they support are also made of sheet steel, cut and welded to create a three-dimensional form which exploits the inherent in-plane stiffness while sufficiently reducing the unsupported areas of plate to avoid local buckling.

Fabricating the ribs and struts from sheet steel at once allows an expression of the structural form – the functions of the individual components and the manufacturing properties of the material – as well as providing an opportunity to display the sculptural quality of exposed joints and members. The art of cutting and welding the steel plate itself becomes part of the architectural vocabulary.

HORIZONTAL

Prague Castle Orangery

Structural engineer   <u>Techniker</u>

Architect   <u>Eva Jiricna Architects</u>

Client   <u>The Czech Rebublic</u>

Prague 1998

This site in the castle gardens had had an orangery since the 15th century. The most recent building, a simple glass greenhouse erected in the 1920s, had been neglected during the communist years in Prague and decayed to the point where replacement was the only option. The brief for the new building was strongly influenced by President Vaclav Havel who wanted a calm retreat, insulated from the pollution in the city (he suffered from asthma), where he could also write his plays. The building also needed to have a strong link with Czech history while being utterly modern.

Eva Jiricna, herself Czech, wanted a structure that would evoke the national

explored. But such an idea is easier to imagine than to execute. A domestic solution, such as seating a post in a hole, may work for a garden fence but would not be satisfactory in a substantial building with a life of many decades. Stresses in a rigid timber connection can be very high and cause local crushing which would quickly lead to the joint becoming loose; also, both rot and corrosion in such a critical detail must be avoided at all costs.

While obviously exploiting to the full the properties of the material, the designers have also conceived the structure of the building to express the very properties that give timber its own unique aesthetic. This structure would look like timber even if it were painted or otherwise disguised. By the shapes, sizes and relative disposition of the elements, the form and manner of the joints between elements and the connections with components of other materials, it is possible to see and understand that the material is timber without having to rely on visual clues from the colour and grain.

Epoxy resin

oprene seal

25 mm titious grout

Glulam timber column

Galvanised R25 bars

12 mm mild steel plate welded to bars

Floor slab

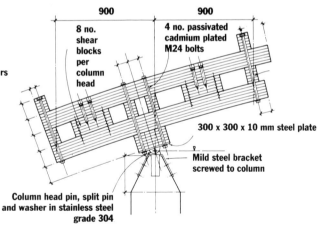

900   900

8 no. shear blocks per column head

4 no. passivated cadmium plated M24 bolts

300 x 300 x 10 mm steel plate

Mild steel bracket screwed to column

Column head pin, split pin and washer in stainless steel grade 304

These various limitations were overcome in the rigid joints at the column bases by using an epoxy resin to glue the timber to corrosion-protected steel rods. These in turn are grouted into the concrete foundations. In this way stress concentrations are avoided by maximising the area over which stresses are transferred between the two materials, and by introducing a tough resin with a modulus lower than both timber and steel to 'attract' the larger proportion

of any deformations.

At the top of each column the problem is inverted: the pin-joint serves to ensure that no bending moments can be transferred from the relatively stiff column to the slender roof members which would otherwise need to be more substantial. The joint detail itself also ensures that loads from the roof are transferred effectively to the full section of the timber without giving rise to high local stresses.

Further reading

AJ Focus, June 1991, pp. 15–19
Patterns, No. 8, Buro Happold, pp. 2–9

Three roof forms   Structural engineer   **Price & Myers**   Architect   **Nicholas Hare Architects**

Felsted School Dining Hall

                                                                 Client   **Felsted School**

Suffolk 1989

The form of roof trusses is influenced by both the architectural design and the loads which they must withstand – the weight of roof covering and wind forces. Wind flowing over a roof causes suction on the leeward slope which can result in considerable uplift on the whole roof structure. The uplift varies with the roof pitch, the building's geographical location and any sheltering it may receive from adjacent buildings. The influence of these loads can be seen in the structure and its form at every level – from the overall roof geometry, the choice of materials, the cross-section of the members, the method and geometry of connections between the members, down to the surface finish left after the manufacture and fabrication of the elements.

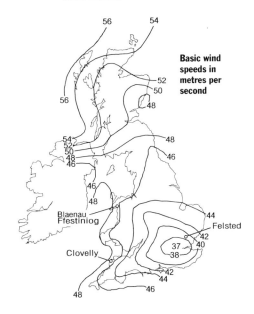

Basic wind speeds in metres per second

A school hall needs to have a presence, and is traditionally a place of quality. The architects wanted to bring as much light as possible into the centre of the room and achieved this by means of a steep pitch with large triangular dormer windows and a warm timber ceiling to reflect the light. The dormer influenced the choice of 6 metres between trusses, but this resulted in an area of roof too great to support elegantly with a timber structure. Instead, a visually lighter-weight structure was created in steel using a combination of hollow sections and rods.

As the building is subject to relatively low wind loads, the steep roof pitch does not lead to excessive horizontal forces on the walls, and the uplift from the wind is never greater than the weight of the roof. The elements of the roof trusses normally acting in tension are, therefore, never subject to load reversal and could be made of very thin rods. The trusses were assembled and adjusted at the tie-rod ends, hidden inside a cylindrical junction box welded to the hollow-section steel strut.

Basic wind speed	39 m/s
Exposure	sheltered (among buildings in open country)
Pitch	42°
Roof dead load	0.80 kN/m²
Maximum suction	-0.80 kN/m²
Net uplift	nil

Further reading

The Architects' Journal, 7 February 1990, pp. 36–43

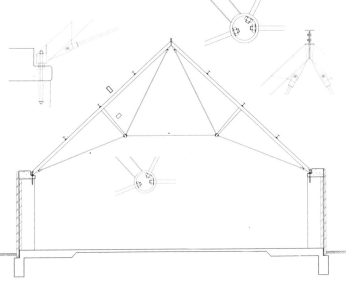

Clovelly Visitors' Centre

Devon 1988

Structural Engineer Price & Myers

Architect Van Heyningen and Haward

Client Clovelly Estate Co Ltd

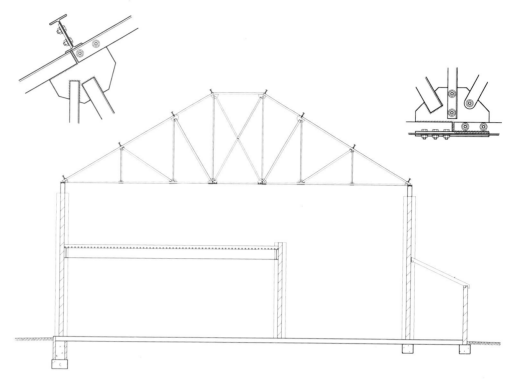

This building is on an exposed site in Devon and subject to very strong prevailing winds. It also has a low-pitched overhanging roof and stands on a cliff top, both of which factors accentuate the effect of the wind.

As the total uplift on this roof can be equivalent to <u>twice</u> its weight, a form of truss had to be found which would, effectively, work equally well upside-down! The purlins are very highly loaded and all the members of the trusses must be able to act as ties in tension and as struts in compression. The architects' wish for a straightforward steel structure was satisfied by a conventional truss made of welded angles and ties which give a sturdy and economical feel to the roof.

Further reading

The Architects' Journal, 31 May 1989, pp. 39–60
Architectural Review, May 1989, pp. 67–69

Basic wind speed	48 m/s
Exposure	high (cliff edge)
Pitch	30°
Roof dead load	0.7 kN/m²
Maximum suction	-1.4 kN/m²
Net uplift	-0.7 kN/m²

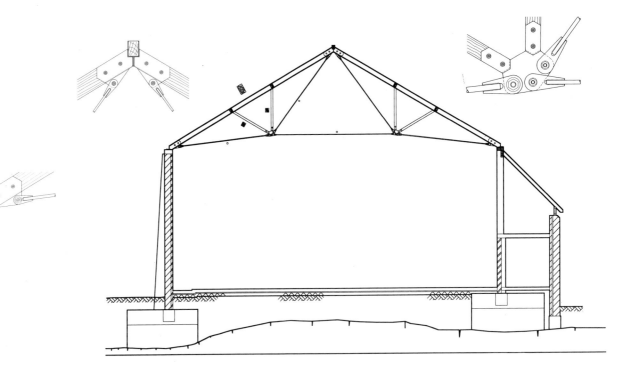

A sports hall is necessarily a plain box because of its function. Here the continuous rooflight provides even illumination and the main visual interest is the roof structure. The architect wanted to use timber where possible and appropriate; the purlins and all the compression members are therefore made of glued laminated timber. The ties and connections are of steel.

The building is subject to quite strong winds and the low pitch leads to relatively high uplift forces on the roof – greater, in fact, than the weight of the roof. In these circumstances the Glulam rafters resist the uplift loads by bending in the opposite direction from normal. There is, however, a complication: the uplift loads also tend to pull the walls together and the slender, steel tie-rods of the trusses are unable to act as struts to resist this. These forces and the lateral wind loads on the building are carried by the buttresses to the walls, which are constructed as cantilevers held firm by the foundations.

The roof structure was made to look considerably lighter by choosing a form for the joints which would express the different material properties of steel and timber (their strengths and their different methods of connection).

A particularly nice detail is the welded joint between the circular tie-rod and the plate which bolts it to the main connection. The eye is drawn to a small D-

Basic wind speed	46 m/s
Exposure	medium (in a small town)
Pitch	30°
Roof dead load	0.75 kN/m^2
Maximum suction	-0.85 kN/m^2
Net uplift	-0.10 kN/m^2

shaped hole which not only assists manufacture, but also forms a large radius of curvature in the notch in the steel plate and thus minimises any stress concentration. This is an effective way of preventing cracks and is especially important in the vicinity of joints where the steel may have been rendered brittle by the welding process.

Further reading

The Architects' Journal, 20 September 1989, pp. 40–47

Channel 4
Headquarters Building

London 1994

Structural engineer   Chris Wise, Adrian Falconer,

Laurence Vye, John White

Ove Arup & Partners

Architect   Richard Rogers & Partners

Specialist glazing contractor   Eiffel, Permasteelisa (UK)

Client   Channel 4

When approaching the entrance to this building, architect and engineer are likely to be struck by the same two features, but perhaps in different ways as a result of their respective perception of form.

To the left of the entrance is a stack of four conference rooms supported by bold, fabricated steel columns and floor beams which meet at pronounced structural pin-joints. The engineer's eye is likely then to look for further means of support since the structure, as it appears, is a mechanism and unstable. Lateral restraint for the stack is, in fact, inherent in the floor plates which can-

tilever out from the main body of the building and act as a horizontal shear structure. The exception is at roof level where a small brace renders the pin-joint rigid and transforms the top storey into a portal frame.

Although there are more obvious ways of stabilising the frame – with cross-bracing or a Vierendeel frame – these would not have created such a vivid architectural and engineering effect.

The main entrance to the building is situated at the base of a 20-metre-high glass wall. This is particularly striking for two reasons: it is made of curved glass plates and appears to lack any means of support. Rather than a vertical structure of steel rods from which the glass panels are hung – the method which has become the norm in glass façades – the glass itself forms part of the load-bearing structure. Each panel is 12 mm thick, measures up to 3 metres x 2.1 metres, and carries the weight of all the panels below.

The entire weight of the glass wall is supported at roof level by three groups of fingers that cantilever off the roof. The engineer wanted the form of the struts in these cantilever structures to reflect their structural function and the way they resist failure by buckling. By fabricating them from steel plate it was possible to create a varying section stiffness (second moment of area) corresponding to the bending resistance which different cross-sections must be able to develop along the length of the strut.

As a geometric form, a third of a cylinder is easy enough to imagine and is a powerful means of focusing attention on the entrance; the idea is not uncommon. But to construct it out of glass is a bold architectural statement and was an intensely complex engineering achievement – made possible only by close collaboration between the architects,

structural engineers and specialist contractors who devised and installed the glazing system. Much of the complexity arose from the fact that the façade is not simply a third of a circle on plan; it also has glass returns at either side. This gives the dramatic effect of the whole foyer area appearing to project out from the concrete-frame building, despite the fact that it is contained in the re-entrant angle between the two main blocks. However, such a projecting façade is far more difficult to support than a glass wall which spans between two parts of a building which can provide firm anchorages.

The glass façade is suspended from sprung supports at roof level. Each panel hangs from the one above by stainless-steel castings at each corner. These also link each panel to its horizontal neighbours. Should one panel fail, shock loads are dissipated by the sprung supports and the weight of the panels below is carried by neighbouring panels, partly by the corner joints and partly by shear in the silicone sealant between the panels.

Alone, however, a series of suspended glass sheets could not withstand wind forces and some means of lateral restraint is necessary. To emphasise the transparency of the wall the bracing structure would need to be located entirely within the narrow foyer and be as visually lightweight as possible.

The challenge was to provide a grid of points, rigidly fixed in space, adjacent to each of the cast-steel brackets and roughly equidistant from them. Since the member connecting the glass to the sta-

bilising structure would have to carry both tension and compression, it could not be a cable. It would have been possible to devise a cable-and-strut scheme to provide the necessary stability, but some of the struts would have needed to be very long, and correspondingly bulky, to prevent buckling.

A prestressed cable-net scheme was proposed which avoided the need for all but very short struts. Horizontal cables following the curve of the glass could be kept taut by a series of vertical cables curved in the opposite sense. In principle this idea was simple enough and, since the steel would be used in tension, the amount of material in the bracing structure could be kept to a minimum. There was just one, rather serious, difficulty: the glass walls that form the returns were at the very places where the horizontal cables might be attached to the building.

In order that the grid of fixed points

could follow the glass surface around the corner at the returns and back to a firm anchor on the main building, the horizontal cables of the cable-net would need to reverse their curvature in the vicinity of the returns. Being a prestressed cable-net, this would entail the vertical cables near the returns passing outside the horizontal cables, adjacent to the glass. In the horizontal plane, these corner cables provide the restraint against which all the other cables are stressed – they have the largest section and curve between floor and ceiling in the opposite sense (inwards) to the vertical cables in the centre of the glass wall.

The complete cable-net consists of seven cables in the vertical plane, pre-

stressed by an orthogonal grid of eight horizontal cables. Perhaps its most striking feature is the large difference in thickness between the horizontal and vertical cables. This arises out of the very way in which a cable-net works as a structure. Its out-of-plane stiffness (perpendicular to the glass) depends on the degree to which the cables are pre-stressed against one another. This in turn depends on two factors: the forces in the cables and their curvature. A certain stiffness can be achieved using a high curvature and small cable tension, or low curvature and high tension. As the radius of curvature of the horizontal cables is typically about 6 metres and so they can be small (between 9 and 11 mm in diameter). The vertical cables have a radius of curvature of about 70 metres and need to be much larger (up to 40 mm) to carry tensions of up to 44 tonnes. They are, nevertheless, loaded well below their capacity of 130 tonnes; this gives ample reserve to prevent any possibility of a fatigue failure resulting from varying wind loads on the façade.

There remained the problem of how to stabilise the free edge at the junction between the curved glass surface and the flat return. After considering a variety of cable and strut restraints, it was finally achieved by exploiting the strut-assisted folded-plate action of the two glass planes: shear forces are carried between the two planes by the silicone sealant.

Further reading

Peter Rice and Hugh Dutton, <u>Le Verre Structurel</u>, Editions du Moniteur, 1990
<u>The Architects' Journal</u>, 20 April 1994, pp. 29–39

Pabellon del futuro

Expo '92

Seville 1992

Structural engineer   Peter Rice, Alistair Lenczner

Ove Arup & Partners

Architect   MBM (Martorell, Bohigas, Mackay)

in association with Jaime Freixa

Client   Expo '92 SA

Stresses in masonry structures, even spectacular ones such as Gothic cathedrals, seldom rise to more than one twentieth of the strength of the stone. Also, the most efficient shape for a free-standing masonry arch is not circular but parabolic (roughly). How, then, to devise a structure that would fully exploit the inherent strength of granite and not rely on sheer weight for its lateral stability, as would befit a 20th-century work of engineering while also referring back to the semi-circular arches of the aqueducts of Roman Spain?

The architects wanted to create a spectacular eastern façade structure to support the roof of the Pavilion of the Future, that would capture the imagination of visitors. Building the façade using natural stone as the primary structural material was seen as an opportunity to challenge contemporary perceptions of stone as purely a cladding or facing material. The result shows how modern analytical, fabrication and construction methods can enable the properties of this ancient building material to be exploited in ways appropriate to our own time.

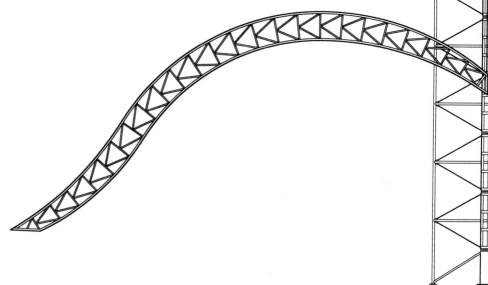

side roof between the outer walls and central flat roof.

By polishing the concrete a marble-like quality was given to the delicate elements; for the more robust elements, sand blasting or tooling was used to give the concrete the appearance of stone building blocks. A variety of connections between the different materials in the floor, wall and roof elements was developed according to how strongly they were to be expressed.

The building thus represents not just a stage in the development of an architect's own work but the collaboration of architect and engineer in developing and refining the use of materials within a particular building system.

Further reading

<u>The Architects' Journal</u>, 1 July 1992, pp. 24–37
<u>Architectural Review</u>, April 1992, pp. 26–33

The Glass House

1992

Structural engineer **Dewhurst Macfarlane and Partners**   Architect **Rick Mather Architects**

At first glance – with the Palm House at Kew in mind, or Glasgow's Kibble Palace or modern structural glazing in façades such as Peter Rice's wall at La Villette – the idea of removing entirely what little metal these structures utilise may not seem an especially significant step to take. They all have a structural system of iron or steel which can carry loads should one or more glass sheets fail. However, to make a structure, no matter how small, entirely of glass demands a totally different approach when calculating the strength of the structure and addressing the safety issues associated with the possibility of failure.

The structural capabilities of glass have long been overlooked, partly, perhaps, because its reputation is coloured by the ease with which a window or wine glass can be broken. Yet a window made of standard 4 mm glass can withstand the force of a hurricane. It is not that glass lacks strength; rather, that its strength can be very variable. It is also prone to sudden and brittle fracture – for this reason suppliers are reluctant to publish strengths for glass. It is now

some 60 years since it was recognised that glass can have a tensile strength approaching that of steel, but it is a strength which is largely lost when the surface of the glass sustains the slightest damage. Even the touch of a soft feather creates microscopic cracks which can propagate with ease and cause a brittle fracture when only a modest stress is applied.

Once recognised, this type of failure could be avoided by encasing freshly drawn glass fibres in a relatively soft resin to form the material now known as fibreglass. The resin serves both to protect the fibres from damage and to prevent them slipping past one another by carrying the shear forces associated with, for instance, bending. The use of a great many fibres has two further structural benefits – the idea of 'safety in numbers' makes it statistically unlikely that more than a few fibres will be weakened by surface damage; and should a crack in the glass start to run, it will be limited to one fibre and not cross the soft resin to adjacent fibres.

Nowadays there are two types of glass that can be used in heavily-loaded glazing – toughened and laminated glass. The former is made by cooling float glass very suddenly during manufacture so that, when finished, the surface is held in compression by the glass inside, which is stressed in tension. Cracks in the surface are thus not subject to tension under moderate bending loads and cannot spread to cause brittle fracture. However, should a crack penetrate the compressed skin, it will propagate freely

through the central tension zone and the glass will shatter in an explosive manner. Laminated glass is made of several layers of float or toughened glass bonded together with a polyester resin. Its effectiveness is based on the same principles as fibreglass.

These ideas were all brought together when considering how glass could be used as a 'normal' load-bearing material in a situation where a real possibility of overloading, a manufacturing flaw or accidental damage, could cause any sheet of glass to crack. Laminated float glass could not be used because it is prone to cracking around holes; neither could a beam of toughened glass because of the catastrophic consequences of a single crack. As is often the case, the solution, with hindsight, was obvious.

Two sheets of toughened glass, each capable of carrying the loads, could be bonded together to form a beam; should one crack, the other could take the load – at least until a new beam could be fitted. But how to join both sheets of the beam to a column? Even if the column were also made of two sheets, the beam would not positively locate with the column and could be easily dislodged. The solution was to increase the number of

sheets to three and the connection could then be made in the manner of a mortice and tenon timber joint. As the glass columns cantilever from ground level, the column-beam junction needs to carry only small loads and, such is the area of overlap, these can be carried by clear silicon rubber. The beams themselves are fish-bellied as a reflection of the larger bending moments towards the centre of the span.

The double glazing for the walls and roof provides the stability for the building by shear-wall action and had to be designed with the different characteristics of toughened and laminated glass – and how they fail – in mind. The final choice was toughened glass for the outer sheet and laminated for the inner. Should the outer sheet shatter on impact with a sharp object, the inner sheet would carry the loads and protect the room's occupants; should a layer of the inner laminate fail, it would be held in

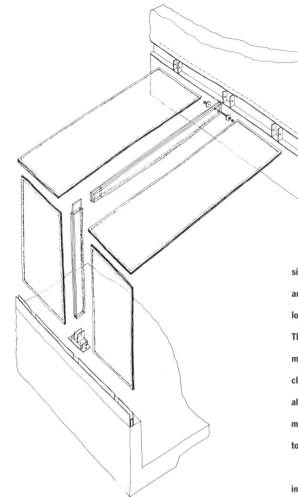

situ by the polymer laminate bonding and the outer sheet would carry the loads until a repair could be effected. The aluminium glazing beads and black mastic normally used in double glazing clearly had to be avoided to achieve an all-glass structure; an air-tight seal was made by bonding the two sheets together with a bead of glass.

The means of avoiding condensation in the sealed glazing unit turned out to yield an unexpected bonus. A Finnish firm was found which could coat glass with a thin layer of metal through which a current can be passed. This acts as a heating element inside the double glazing and prevents condensation. So effective was this technology that it was also able to provide most of the heating for the entire all-glass extension.

Further reading

The Architects' Journal, 22 July 1992, pp. 40–43
AJ Focus, July 1992, pp. 119–211
Architectural Review, February 1993, pp. 67–70

Entertainment complex, Cribbs Causeway

Bristol 1999

Structural engineer	Structures 1		Architect	Faulkner Browns
Membrane contractor	Architen		Client	Prudential & J.T. Baylis

The architect's vision for the entrance to this commercial out-of-town entertainment complex was a membrane canopy supported by a large timber arch to break down the rectangular features of the main building. Membrane canopies like this are usually procured through design-and-build membrane subcontractors, and tenders are usually invited on the basis of little more than the architect's concept sketch. Since membrane contractors' skills have developed out of the marine sail-making and rigging industries, they often choose to collaborate with structural engineers when a project demands the creative and technical skills which engineers are best able to provide. Such a collaboration between Structures 1 and Architen produced a highly visible realisation of the architect's original vision. Their scheme interpreted the basic idea of the arch in line with the geometric and statical constraints of the membrane to create a unique architectural element, with its

own structural aesthetic and bespoke vocabulary of construction details.

The architect wanted the four cusps of the membrane canopy to be supported from five points around the circumference of the arch. A timber arch sufficiently stiff to carry the cable loads from the membrane would have needed to be very large indeed. To achieve an arch with the slender form and dimensions preferred by the architect, the full arc could be broken down into short lengths to achieve sufficient resistance to buckling. These short lengths forming

a seven-pin arch would, in turn, need to be connected at a series of nodes and the whole then braced to give overall stability, not unlike the vertebrae in our spine. The parabolic form of the arch corresponds to the funicular shape for the applied loads, which minimises the size of the stabilising structure. In-plane stability is provided by two structural systems – a truss on the extrados and cable-bracing along chords on the intrados. Together these provide an attractive

asymmetry to the arch and less 'visual noise' in the void between membrane and arch. Out-of-plane stability was arranged by using a pair of arches braced by struts between them and the truss on the extrados.

The parabolic arch was assembled on the ground and raised into its inclined position when the membrane was attached. The final pre-tension in the membrane is provided, in part, using the weight of the arch itself, creating a double structural counterpoise between the arch and membrane.

Aviary

Munich Zoo 1980

Structural engineer **Buro Happold**

Architect **Jorg Gribl with Frei Otto**

Client **Tierpark AG**

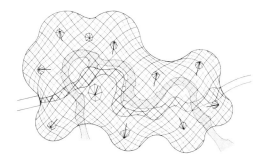

The architect's vision for an aviary to cover about 4500 square metres was 'a structure like a cloud'. The interior should be impeded by as little structure as possible and the boundary surface should allow small birds (and wind) to pass through freely, but be a barrier to large birds and predators.

Throughout the project two strands of design development progressed simultaneously, with ideas constantly passing from one to the other. A form had to be found which satisfied both architectural and structural constraints, and suitable materials, connections and construction processes had to be evolved which would enable the form to be built.

The idea of using a steel mesh as the material of the boundary surface presented itself early on, but it was not clear how such a net might withstand snow loads of up to 0.4 kN/m². The original idea of hanging a lightweight mesh beneath a grid of taut cables was abandoned because it was felt it would look rather 'baggy' in the snowy conditions that Munich often experiences. Better would be a taut net which could somehow carry these imposed loads by stretching like an elastic sheet; but a mesh of steel wires strong enough to carry the forces would be too stiff to give the desired elasticity. And then a solution was noticed, literally within sight of the proposed aviary: a mesh made of crimped steel wires as used in some of the animal cages elsewhere in the zoo.

Not only would a mesh of crimped wires have the right stress/strain characteristics for the elastic net, it would

also provide adequate safety should the mesh be overloaded beyond the steel's elastic limit, since it could deform easily in a plastic manner while retaining adequate strength. And, finally, the crimping prevents the wires sliding past one another so that the holes in the mesh do not become enlarged.

Most importantly, the crimped mesh would be able to sustain large in-plane shear deformations with little resistance. This property is essential in a tensioned cable structure since it is by this means that a net is able to find its own shape when stretched over a number of supports. Nevertheless, the angle of shear has to be limited to about 40° otherwise the net goes slack in one direction and produces unsightly folds which permanently deform a material such as steel.

Having devised a suitable 'material' for the boundary surface there were several further matters to resolve. How could the mesh be made to take up a shape which would satisfy the architect's vision of a free-form geometry while being taut enough to work as an

elastic sheet and not be vibrated by the wind like the fabric of a conventional tent? How would the homogenous mesh be supported from just a few points without causing unacceptable stress concentrations? How would a continuous net of some 5000 square metres be manufactured and erected? And, not least, how would the precise form of the net be established and defined and its structural performance and safety confirmed. In other words, how would it be designed?

By suspending the mesh from a number of masts any number of suitable forms for the boundary surface could be created. Its profile could be controlled in several ways, depending on the number, position and height of the masts, the use of tie-downs at points between the

masts and the precise shape of the unsheared mesh. Once a form had been created, and because the surface would be anticlastic (doubly-curved in opposing directions), the net could be tensioned by fixing it down around the perimeter and at the tie-downs, and by tightening the cables that tie the net to the mastheads. By this means of pre-stressing, sufficient tension could be introduced into the net to limit its movement when buffeted by the wind.

It was first proposed to overcome the problem of stress concentrations in the net at the mast supports by means of a mushroom head, supported in turn by cables from the mast top. This idea would have avoided a major perforation of the mesh but was abandoned because of anticipated difficulties during construction and the need to erect the aviary over a mature ash tree. An alternative system was devised using a pantograph system of cables and linked mesh-clamps. These collect the load from every mesh filament around the perimeter of a roughly circular hole in the net and concentrate them into just four adjustable cables attached to each masthead. The hole is 'patched' and a seal around the mast effected by a section of unstressed mesh.

The woven mesh of 3.2 mm crimped stainless-steel wires was available in rolls 2.5 metres wide, and sections of mesh were pre-assembled in the factory into rolls 12.5 metres wide and 40 or 50 metres long. This was only made possible by using the newly developed argon shield technology (TIG) to butt-weld the stainless steel wires – sixteen for every metre of edge. These larger sections were welded together on site before being lifted into position.

For the architect the form of the structure was only constrained by its function, the site and his vision. For the structural engineer the form was constrained also by how it might work as a structure, and how he might be able to justify this expectation. The first stage in this process was to make a number of models of the aviary to help visualise and develop its architectural form and its structural concept, form and behaviour. These models were invaluable in experimenting with the geometry of the complex curved surface and seeing how the masts and tie-downs might be best arranged.

While small models are invaluable in generating forms and can demonstrate that the overall structural concept is sound, they are of limited help to the engineer when it comes to matters of detail. Such models are dangerously misleading in many crucial respects – model struts and ties are disproportionately strong and stiff, and a model net has elastic and shearing properties that are not at all representative of a full-size steel cable net. Such inherent difficulties in scaling up forces and deformations on a small model to a full-size tension structure mean that they cannot provide the engineer with an adequate justification of the expected behaviour of the structure. A further problem is that the geometry of this class of structure is a naturally generated form and not one which can be described by a mathematical equation, as is the case with a cylindrical or hyperbolic-paraboloid shell. In order for engineers to analyse the forces in a structure, they must be able to describe the form mathematically.

Finding the precise geometry and forces in a simple tension structure such as a chain is not at all difficult. The principal complexity in a cable net is the sheer number of mathematical equations to solve, and this was only made economically possible as the power of computers grew. For a flexible tension surface the forces and stresses in the system depend upon its geometry, and vice versa: an iterative approach is therefore called for. A surface geometry is specified, based on approximate measurements taken from the small models and hand calculations, and the forces are computed. Any out-of-balance forces tend to deform the (computer) model to a new geometry, which is then taken as the start of a new calculation

cycle, and so on, until an equilibrium state is reached. In this manner the equilibrium shape and forces in the net and supports can be found for the many different combinations of static, prestressing, wind and snow loads.

With the development of this approach to designing tension structures, another possibility arose. The geometrical model of the cable net generated by the computer could help define with great accuracy the dimensions of the flat areas of mesh that would need to be 'stitched' together along their edges, and of the many cables and masts in the structure. In this way the need for adjustable masts and cables, equivalent to the guy ropes of a conventional tent, could be avoided and an altogether more elegant appearance achieved.

Further reading

Patterns, No. 5, Buro Happold, 1989, pp. 29–32
Structural Engineering Review, July 1994

Peninsula Building

Structural engineer <u>RFR</u>

Architect <u>Paul Andreu</u>

Roissy Airport, Paris 1999

Client <u>Aéroports de Paris</u>

It is not uncommon for an architect's dream of transparency or simplicity or homogeneity to be sacrificed in the design development process under the influence of practical issues such as manufacturing and assembly methods, building regulations, expansion joints or lack of time. It needs a determined architect, persistent, conscientious and skilled engineers and, of course, an enlightened client to allow the full potential of the construction industry to show itself.

The scale and form of the two new peninsulas at Roissy's Terminal 2F had been established by client and architect in 1993. Progress towards the final solution by RFR was able to proceed slowly and both the concept design and development of details were able to benefit from many iterations. The result is an elegance that is seldom found in a building enclosing such an enormous volume – 200 metres long, tapering from 50 to 13 metres in span and reaching a maximum height of 22 metres.

The structure has no expansion joints. The entire building is attached to the Main Concourse building at just one point – the end of the spine, or blade as it was nicknamed – through which are carried horizontal loads from wind and the trusses at the outer end of the building. Each of the 50 pairs of ribs can move ±60 mm in the direction of the blade. As temperatures change the envelope moves like our rib cage when we breathe. The structure derives its lateral stability from the concrete concourse structure to which each rib is attached with tension rods in bicycle-wheel fashion. The bottom of each rib rests on a cantilever, which is hinged on a vertical axis to allow the horizontal movement relative to the concourse.

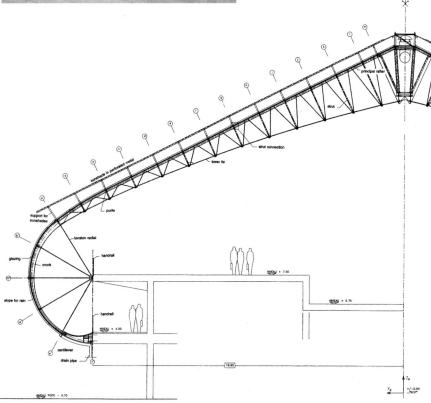

'Engineering and Architecture' Architectural Design Profile 70. Architectural Design, Vol. 57, 11/12, 1987

A special issue celebrating the engineer's contribution to architecture. Several thought-provoking essays from Ted Happold, Charles Jenks, Jack Zunz, Robert Thorne and Derek Walker, inter alia, and photo-essays on a number of current projects.

Form Force Mass 3: Structures – a proposal for the classification and description of structures by Frei Otto. Report no. IL23 of Institute of Lightweight Structures, University of Stuttgart, 1992.

A remarkable condensation of the entire subject of structures into one small volume, in which understanding about structures is derived and conveyed by means of the process of devising a structure for our knowedge about structures.

Jean Prouvé: complete works by Peter Sulzer, Birkhäuser, Basel, Vol. 1, 1997, Vol. 2, 2000

All structural engineers should know Prouvé. He united a sculptor's feel for materials and form with the practicality of manufacture and assembly. For example, he developed the lightweight cladding for buildings in the 1930s and he was using structural aluminium with elegance in the early 1950s.

Light structures, structures of light: the art and engineering of tensile architecture by Horst Berger. Birkhäuser, Basel, 1996

Like the classic works by Nervi, Torroja and Rice, this book has special importance for being not only written by an eminent practising engineer, but by one who goes far beyond merely writing about his own remarkable works.

'The Nature of Engineering' by E. (Ted) Happold. Gold Medal Address. The Structural Engineer, Vol. 70, October, 1992, pp. 349–354

A compact discussion of what structural engineers do and should do better in order to increase their status, influence and prosperity.

Owen Williams by David Cottam. Architectural Association, London 1986

The story of one of Britain's few acknowledged engineer/architects who exploited the richness and versatility of concrete. He is remembered mainly as engineer for the buildings at the Wembley British Empire Exhibition (1924) and engineer/architect of several memorable buildings during the 1930s – the Dorchester Hotel, the Empire Pool at Wembley, the Peckham Health Centre, the Boot's and Daily Express buildings. He also designed the first bridges on the M1 motorway.

The Philosophy of Structures by Eduardo Torroja. University of California Press 1967

Still a classic in our field, unfortunately long out of print. He was a rare combination of imaginative engineer and someone who could abstract generalities from his own particular experiences and present them as the principles that guided his engineering life. Although written in the golden age of concrete and shells, he talks equally passionately about steel and timber, and all manner of structural forms. This book is unique amongst the writings of engineers in not focusing on his own works. For those, the reader should go to The Structures of Eduardo Torroja, F.W. Dodge Corporation, 1958. For one of the most remarkable uses of a thin concrete shell, try his Pont de Suert church.

'The ship that found herself', A Day's Work by Rudyard Kipling, London, Macmillan, 1980

The only example I know of structural engineering written from the point of view of the structure itself! The wrought-iron plates and rivets of a ship tell their own story of the stresses and strains they must endure while surviving a transatlantic journey and a great storm. In the same volume, 'The Bridge Builder' is another rare example of engineering in literature.

Structural and Civil Engineering Design, edited by William Addis. Vol. 12 of series 'Studies in the History of Civil Engineering', ariorum/Ashgate, 1999

This book is one of a dozen in the series which reprint about 20 of the best articles on engineering history written during the twentieth century, prefaced by an introduction and bibliography. The others in the series are worth consulting, too; they focus on certain types of structure (e.g. dams, Gothic cathedrals) and certain materials (e.g. concrete, cast and wrought iron, timber).

Structural Engineering: the Nature of Theory and Design by William Addis. Ellis Horwood, Chichester, 1990

Here I discuss the nature of structural engineering design as an activity, an art undertaken by skilled people, and trace how it has been, or might have been done during the last two millennia. I look at the nature of progress in engineering and the contribution which engineering science ('theory') has played in the work of the design engineer. I have tried to provide for engineering with something analogous to the long established 'history and philosophy of science'. It contains an extensive bibliography.

Structural Use of Glass in Buildings, Institution of Structural Engineers, London, 1999

Not only a useful guide to the unfamiliar world of structural elements made with glass, this is a rare example of a book that approaches structural engineering from the point of view of the design engineer, combining principles and materials science with design guidance and manufacturing issues, and illustrated by eye-catching examples.

The Tower and the Bridge by David Billington. Princeton University Press, 1985

The book traces what the author claims is 'the new art of structural engineering' (the book's subtitle) from Telford through to the present day. It is a brief but excellent introduction to many of the structural engineers whose work is worth scrutiny, though the impact of the book is reduced by uninspiring black and white photographs. Many useful references.

The Turning Point of Building: Structure and Design by Konrad Wachsmann. New York, Reinhold, 1961

This seminal book (translated from the German original) charts the development of industrialisation in building from the Crystal Palace onwards. Wachsmann was neither architect nor engineer, but, like Jean Prouvé, a craftsman who transcended all boundaries.

Zen and the Art of Motorcycle Maintenance by Robert M. Pirsig. Bodley Head, 1974

Surely one of the best book titles ever. In charting a voyage of personal and psychological discovery, the author builds upon engineering skills he has acquired and the relationship between his intellectual and physical experience of materials and mechanics.

Name Index

Subject Index

Acknowledgements

I am grateful, most of all, to the many engineers and firms who have given their time and energy to help me tell something of the engineering stories of their buildings; without their enthusiasm there would have been no book. Any errors in the text, however, are mine, not theirs.

Especial thanks are due to Tess, Orlando and Oscar who have tolerated my absence every time I disappeared off to the computer to do yet another bit of book.

I am also indebted to Frank Newby who sadly died recently, with whom I shared and developed my enthusiasm for structural engineering, old and new, for more than twenty years.

Illustration credits

Where appropriate, illustrations are credited from left to right and from top to bottom of each page.

Page 1–14: Bill Addis (BA) except page 2 extreme right, Beat Kasper; page 10, Horst Berger; extreme right Peter Durant; page 11 top right, Ove Arup & Partners (OAP); second from right, Heini Schneebeli

page 14: Portuguese National Pavilion, Lisbon, OAP (Andrew Minson); Ecozentrum OAP (Peter Ross); ChekLapKok, OAP (Colin Wade).

page 17: Chris Wise; Chris Wise; OAP; OAP

page 18: Chris Wise

page 19: photographs Richard Davies; sketch Sir Norman Foster

page 20, 21: photograph Richard Davies; drawings Sir Norman Foster & Partners; sketch Sir Norman Foster

page 23–25: OAP

page 26: elevation and section Sir Norman Foster & Partners; other drawings OAP

page 27: Sir Norman Foster & Partners; BA; OAP

page 28: OAP; Peter Mackinven, OAP

page 29: Jane Richardson; OAP

page 30: OAP; OAP

page 31: drawing Tony Hunt; photograph YRM-Anthony Hunt Associates

page 32: computer image Mike Barnes; photographs YRM-AHA

page 33 - 34: Peter Mackinven, OAP

page 35: Schlaich Bergermann & Partners

page 36: Schlaich Bergermann & Partners

page 37: Peter Mackinven, OAP

page 38: OAP; OAP; Richard Davies

page 39: photographs BA; drawing OAP

page 40: photographs Ben Johnson; drawings BA

page 41: Chris Wise; Ben Johnson

page 42: BA

page 44: Tony Copeland; Heinz Isler; Tony Copeland; BA; Tony Copeland

page 45: Tony Copeland; Heinz Isler; Tony Copeland

page 46: Anthony Hunt Associates

page 47: C.V. Buchan Ltd.

page 48 Buro Happold; Dennis Gilbert

page 49: Ben Morris; Buro Happold; Dennis Gilbert; Buro Happold;

page 50: CAD

page 51: Buro Happold

page 52, 53: OAP

page 54: Schlaich Bergermann & Partners; BA

page 55: BA; Buro Happold; Michael Hopkings & Partners; Buro Happold; Buro Happold; Michael Hopkings & Partners

page 56: drawings BA; photograph Buro Happold

page 57: BA; BA; BA; Buro Happold; Buro Happold

page 58: photographs Lauren Camber, Wilkinson Eyre Architects; drawings Bison Structures Ltd.

page 59: Owens Corning

page 60: drawing Price & Myers; Heini Schneebeli; BA

page 61: drawings BA; Heini Schneebeli

page 62, 63: drawings BA; photographs Doug Allan, British Antarctic Survey

page 64: Heini Schneebeli; BA; Price & Myers

page 66, 67: photographs Peter Cook; drawings Short Ford & Associates

page 68: Short Ford & Associates; Short Ford & Associates; BA; YRM-AHA

page 69: drawings Symonds Travers Morgan; photographs David Tasker; Oasis Forest Holiday Villages.

page 70: Kurt Gahler

page 71: Robert Keiser; Kurt Gahler

page 72, 73: Arup Associates

page 74: Crispin Boyle, Arup Associates; Arup Associates; Arup Associates

page 75: Harris & Sutherland; BA; MacCormac Jamieson Prichard & Wright; Harris & Sutherland; Phil Cooper

page 76 Peter Mackinven; OAP; BA

page 77: drawings OAP; photograph BA

page 78: drawing Price & Myers; photographs Heini Schneebeli

page 79: drawings Price & Myers; photographs BA; Heini Schneebeli

page 80: drawings BA; photographs Laing Management Ltd

page 81, 82: drawing BA; CAD images Buro Happold; photograph RHWL Architects

page 84: photographs Vallode et Pistre et Associes; OAP; BA

page 85: Mike Banfi; Vallode et Pistre et Associes; Mike Banfi

page 86: BA

page 87: Phil Cooper

page 88–91: photographs BA; drawings Buro Happold

page 92, 93: photographs Curtins Consulting Engineers; drawings BA

page 94 YRM-AHA; Laing Management Limited

page 95: Peter Cook; YRM-AHA

page 96: drawings & CAD image Anthony Hunt Associates; photographs Sir Robert McAlpine

page 98: BA

page 99: Ian Lambot

page 100: BA; Ben Johnson; OAP

page 102: drawings Marc Mimram; photographs BA

page 103: Marc Mimram; BA; photographs BA

page 104, 105: Techniker; Eva Jiricna Architects

page 106: ABM Consulting Engineers, BA

page 107: ABM Consulting Engineers, BA

page 108, 109: Buro Happold

page 110: drawings Price & Myers; photographs Martin Charles

page 111, 112: drawings Price & Myers; photographs Heini Schneebeli

page 113–115: BA

page 116: photographs BA; drawings OAP

page 117: BA; Alistair Lenzner; OAP; Bruce Danziger

page 118: OAP

page 120: BA; Peter Mackinven; OAP

page 121: Peter Mackinven

page 122, 123: photographs BA; drawings Dewhurst Macfarlane & Partners

page 124: FaulknerBrowns; Structures 1

page 125: drawings Buro Happold; photograph Robert Thorne

page 126: Buro Happold; Jorg Gribbl; Mike Barnes

page 127: Buro Happold; Mike Barnes; BA

page 128, 129: RFR

page 130: Schlaich Bergermann & Partners

page 131–133: drawings OAP; photographs BA